The
Best
Craft Book Ever

Jane Bull

More than 200 projects from Jane Bull's best-selling craft books

A Penguin Company
LONDON, NEW YORK, MUNICH,
MELBOURNE, AND DELHI

DESIGN • Jane Bull
TEXT • Penelope Arlon, Caroline Green
PHOTOGRAPHY • Andy Crawford
DESIGN ASSISTANCE • Sadie Thomas,
Gemma Fletcher
EDITORIAL ASSISTANCE • Deborah Lock

PUBLISHING MANAGER • Sue Leonard
MANAGING ART EDITOR • Rachael Foster
PRODUCTION • Angela Graef
DTP DESIGNER • Almudena Díaz

For Charlotte, Billy, and James

First American Edition, 2006

Published in the United States by DK Publishing, Inc.
375 Hudson Street, New York, New York 10014

07 08 09 10 10 9 8 7 6 5 4 3 2

Published in Great Britain by Dorling Kindersley Limited.

A catalog record for this book is available
from the Library of Congress

ISBN-13: 978-0-7566-2236-7

Color reproduction by GRB Editrice S.r.l., Verona, Italy
Printed and bound in China by Toppan

Contains material from The Crafty Art Book, The Rainy
Day Book, The Sunny Day Book, The Gardening Book,
The Magic Book, The Halloween Book, Change Your
Room, The Party Book, The Christmas Book, The Merry
Christmas Activity Book, and Sticker Activity Books:
Fairy World, Parties, Dinosaur, Gifts and Cards

discover more at
www.dk.com

Ha Ha

Contents

A crafty book of arty ideas . . .

Get crafty with your art

Crafty kit • Here's a guide to the materials

Paper or cardboard?

TRACING PAPER • You will need tracing paper for the Pirate Pete templates; however, parchment paper is a great alternative.

TISSUE PAPER • Tissue paper is the best paper for the roses.

PAPER • Normal, everyday paper can be used for the marble and other printing techniques.

CARD • Folded boxes can be made with paper or very thin posterboard. Paper is easier to fold and surprisingly sturdy. Thin posterboard is best for woolly web bases and for cards and tags.

Tissue paper

Paints and pens

POSTER PAINT • It is a good all-around paint for posterboard and paper. It is cheap and easy to use. For printing paper, use poster paint.

OIL PAINT • When you make the marble paper, you will need to use oil paint. You will also need some turpentine—ask your parents to help you with this.

FABRIC PENS • When you use fabric pens to decorate Pirate Pete, follow the instructions on the packet for best results.

Poster paint

Bits and pieces

To finish off your projects nicely, you will often need odds and ends. Keep a lookout at home for things that are about to be thrown away and start collecting for your arty crafts. Look for items such as:

- Buttons and beads
- Ribbon
- Old paper
- Things to print

with, like empty thread spools, used-up pens, old sponges, and anything else with good texture.

⭐ **Ask an adult.** You will see this sign if you need to ask an adult to help you.

Scissors

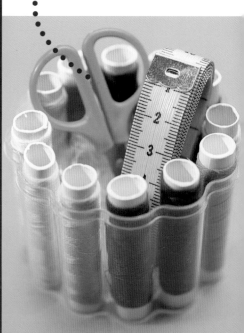

4

used to make the projects in this book.

Pins and needles

WOOL • For the knitting, woolly webs, and the cross-stitch, you will need yarn.

DARNING NEEDLE • If you are sewing with yarn, you will need a darning needle.

KNITTING NEEDLES • Knitting needles come in different sizes, so make sure you don't get ones that are too fat or thin.

SEWING NEEDLE • For sewing with thin thread, you will need a sewing needle with a small eye—not a darning needle. If you have trouble threading a needle, you can buy a cheap tool to make it easier.

PINS • Always pin material before you sew it.

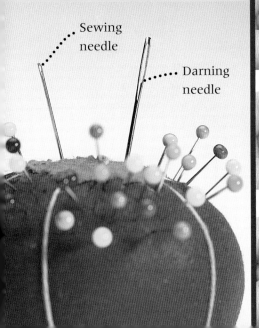

Sewing needle

Darning needle

Back stitch

This is a handy stitch to learn—it's quick yet strong and was used to stitch up Pirate Pete on page 9 to keep his filling from falling out. It's a bit like a doubled-up running stitch.

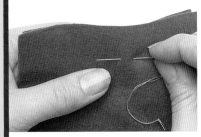

Knot the end of the thread. Push the needle down and up through the fabric.

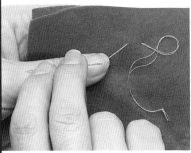

Pull the needle all the way through to the knot.

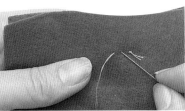

Place the needle between the knot and the dangling thread.

Bring the needle up ahead of the dangling thread.

Repeat these steps and sew over a few stitches to finish off.

Fabrics

EMBROIDERY FABRIC • In order to make the cross-stitch patterns, you will have to buy special fabric called aida cloth. It has big holes that you can easily pull yarn through.

COTTON FABRIC • For Pirate Pete and friends, plain cotton, such as some old sheet material, is the best to use. Otherwise any old scraps of white cotton will do.

Beads for noses

Buttons for eyes

Handy hints and tips

Be prepared! Collect bits and pieces regularly, like the things all around this page, so that you have lots to work with.

Start collecting today!

All about glue

Glue stick   Wallpaper paste   All-purpose glue

Wallpaper paste

You can buy this paste in bags from any home improvement store. Put about a tablespoon of the flakes into a bowl and add water until it blends in. It should be thick enough to brush onto a surface.

Glue stick

This is a very clean glue and is best for paper, since it won't make it crinkle.

All-purpose glue

This is not only a strong glue, it also smells strong. Use it for gluing cardboard pieces together.

PVA glue (Elmer's glue)

PVA is very useful glue for fabric and cardboard. Mixed with a bit of water, it is a good varnish, and mixed with paint, it will give the colored surface a shiny finish.

Threading a needle

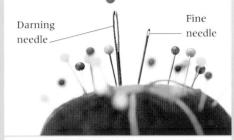

Darning needle   Fine needle

This gadget helps you thread a needle. You can get them in any store that sells thread.

Push the fine wire through the eye.

Push the needle down to the metal.   Thread your yarn through the wire.

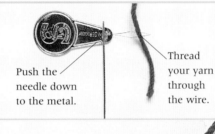

Now just pull the threader and the needle apart and you've done it—easy!

Keep on pulling, and then remove the wire threader.

Sewing back stitch

Knot the end of the thread and push the needle down and up through the fabric.

Pull the needle all the way through to the knot.

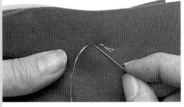

Place the needle between the knot and the dangling thread.

Bring the needle up ahead of the dangling thread.

Repeat these steps and sew over a few stitches to finish off.

Get weaving
(page 23)
Quick start and finish

If you have trouble getting your weaving started, use sticky tape to hold the wool in place.

Tape the yarn to the back of the plate.

Turn the plate over and wind the wool as on page 23.

When you are finished, turn the plate over.

Tape the other end.

Make and Create

Get crafty with your art

Pirate Pete

Yo, ho, ho, it's a pirate's life for me! How would you like to be drawn, sewn, and stuffed? That's how I'm made.

Land ho!

Shiver me beanbags

This jolly pirate is stuffed full of rice. You can use any dried food, such as lentils, popcorn, dried beans, or small pasta. Don't stuff it too full, however—it needs to be a bit floppy.

Meet the gang

"All aboard the Jolly Roger!" shouts Pete to his crew. He couldn't sail his ship without his trusted beanbag friends. "Hoist the sails, raise the anchor, we're off to find the hidden treasure!"

Beanbag tips

Pete's pattern can be used to make the crew, too. Just add extra ears for the animals, yarn braids for the girls, and leave out the legs for the ghosts and snowman.

Whoo hoooo

Follow the lines and dots

The hard line shows you where you cut the material, and the dotted line shows you where to sew.

Include these ears for cat shape.

Leave a space here to fill up your toy.

TRACING PAPER

PEN

SCISSORS

Pirate pattern

Sew along this line.

Cut out along this line.

Snip away these diamond shapes from the material. This will help the material to turn inside out neatly.

Place a piece of tracing paper over this page and draw around the outline that you have chosen. Cut the shape out.

Cut straight along here for ghost or snowman shapes.

Throw together Pete

Pirate Pete is ready to set sail

on the high seas. Use the template from page 11 to make Pirate Pete and go on to throw together his whole crew. "Ha, ha, me hearties!"

Your pirate kit

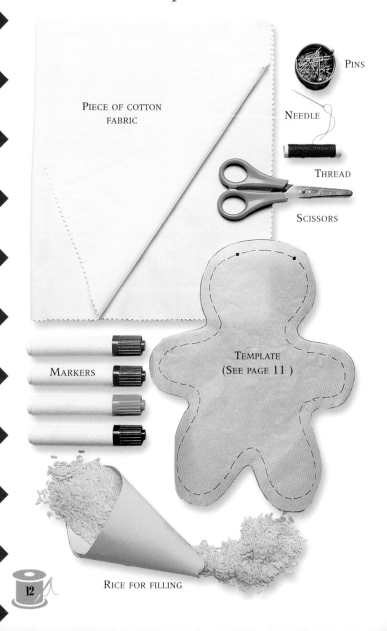

PINS

PIECE OF COTTON
FABRIC

NEEDLE

THREAD

SCISSORS

MARKERS

TEMPLATE
(SEE PAGE 11)

RICE FOR FILLING

I

Cut out the shape

Lay the Pete template on a piece of material that is fold in half. Cut it out. You will now have two Pete shape

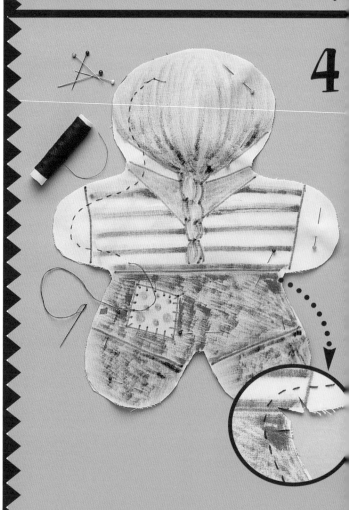

4

Sew all the way around

Use small stitches to sew around the pirate. Leave a small gap at the top.

2

Draw Pirate Pete

Color the front of Pete on one piece and draw the back of him on the other.

3

Pin the pieces together

Place the right sides of Pete together and pin them.

5

Turn him inside out

You should now see the right sides of Pete on the outside.

Curl a piece of paper into a tube funnel for easy filling.

When you have filled Pete, fold the open edges inward, pin them together, and sew the opening up.

6

Fill him up

Fill Pirate Pete up with a dried food, such as rice or beans, and sew him up!

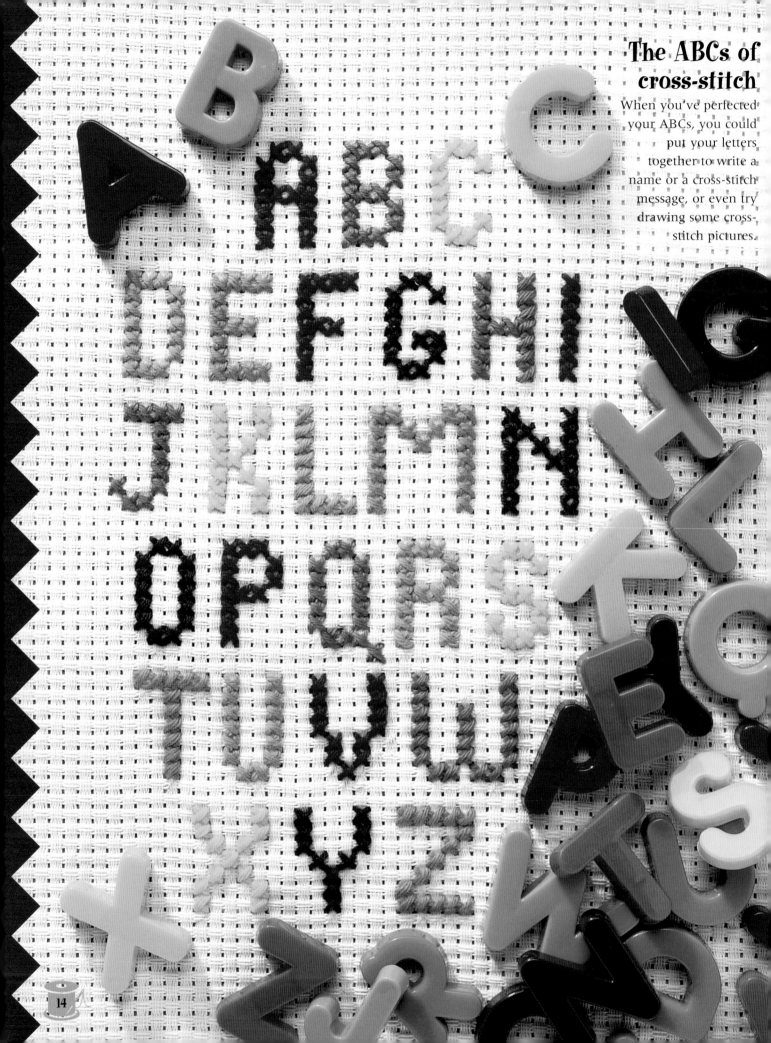

The ABCs of cross-stitch

When you've perfected your ABCs, you could put your letters together to write a name or a cross-stitch message, or even try drawing some cross-stitch pictures.

Cross-stitch

Simple samplers are as easy as A, B, C. Crisscross, crisscross, and create pictures.

Following guide lines

• It helps to draw out the area you want to sew as small squares—each square is one cross-stitch.
• To keep your letters the same size, base them on the same number of squares across and up—for example, 7 squares down and 4 squares across.
• Remember, a curving part of a letter still has to be drawn using the squares.

Don't make the line too dark or it will show when sewn.

Pencil

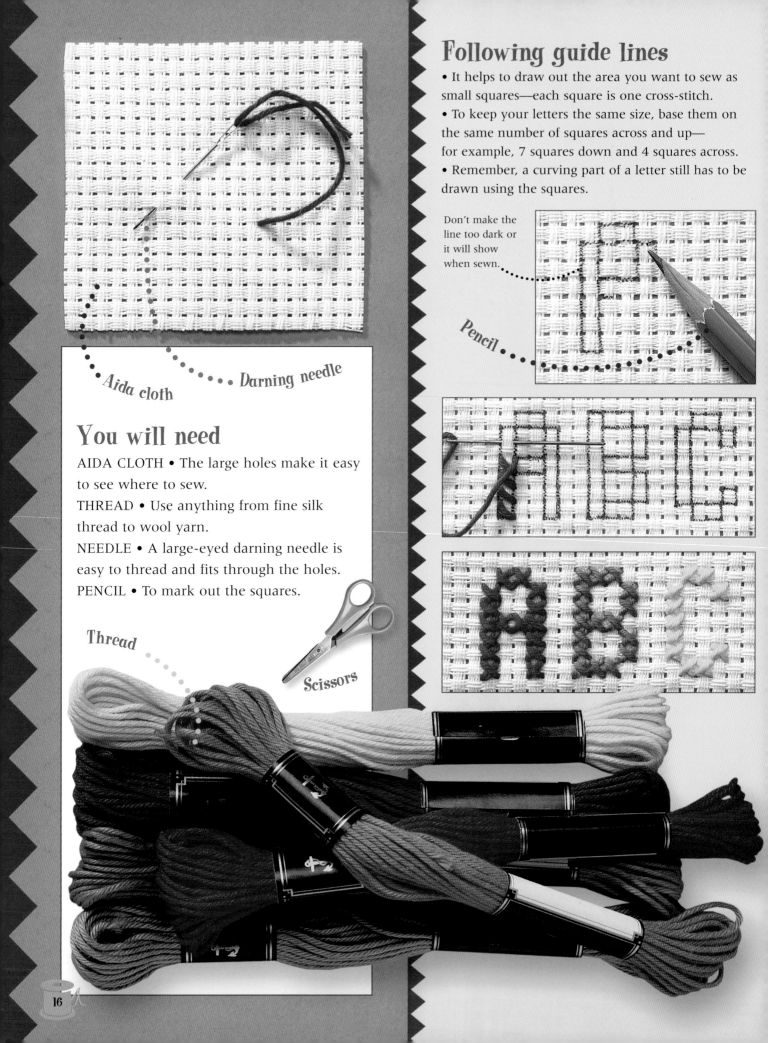

Aida cloth • *Darning needle*

You will need

AIDA CLOTH • The large holes make it easy to see where to sew.

THREAD • Use anything from fine silk thread to wool yarn.

NEEDLE • A large-eyed darning needle is easy to thread and fits through the holes.

PENCIL • To mark out the squares.

Thread

Scissors

Single stitch

For one stitch, use a short length of thread and don't forget to knot the end.

Stitches in a row

To sew a row, sew a few stitches one way, then go back the other way.

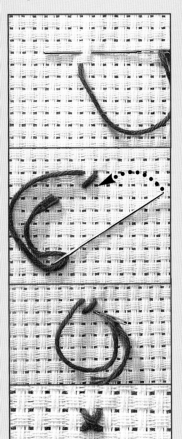

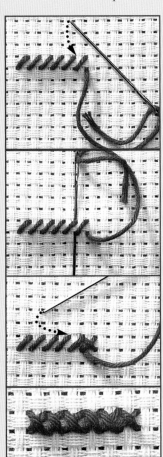

Back view and finishing off

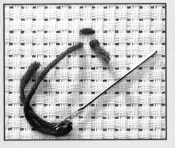

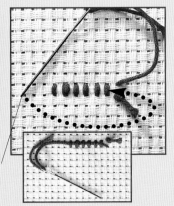

Finish a stitch on the back and thread it through some stitches to secure it.

A·B·C Cross-stitch letter squares

Once you have learned to cross-stitch, you can experiment with all sorts of different patterns and colors. Try these single letters. Cut a square of fabric about 18 holes by 18 holes. Draw on the areas in pencil, and stitch away.

Try fraying the edges of your work by pulling away the first few strands of the fabric.

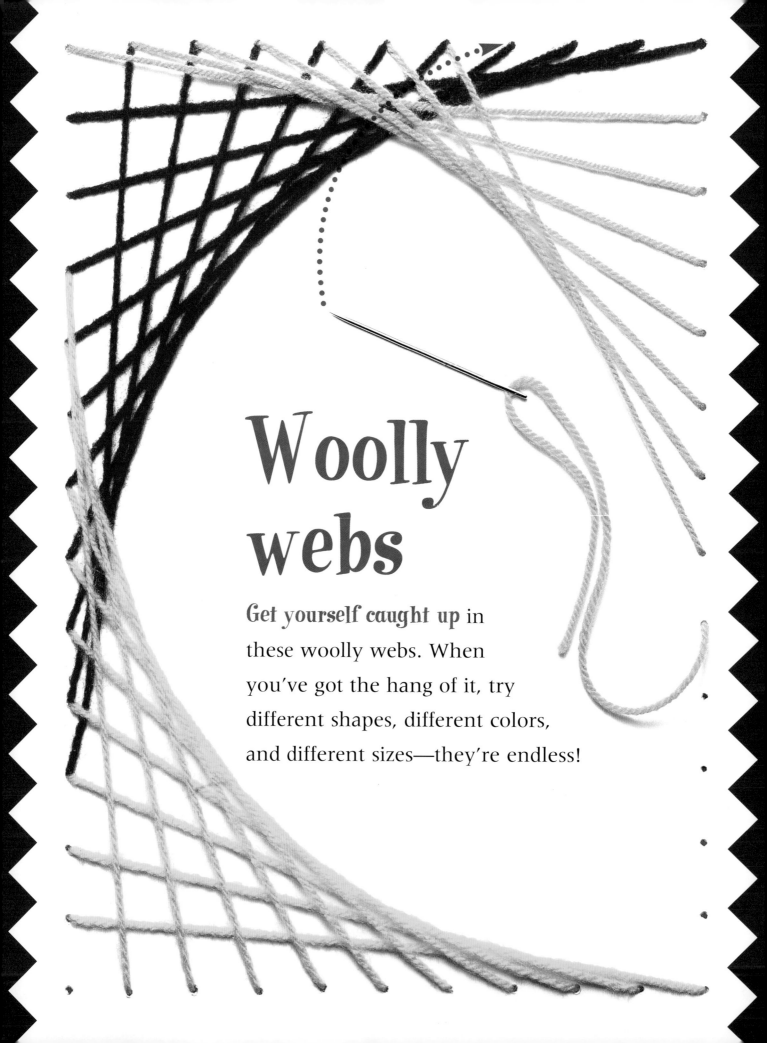

Woolly webs

Get yourself caught up in these woolly webs. When you've got the hang of it, try different shapes, different colors, and different sizes—they're endless!

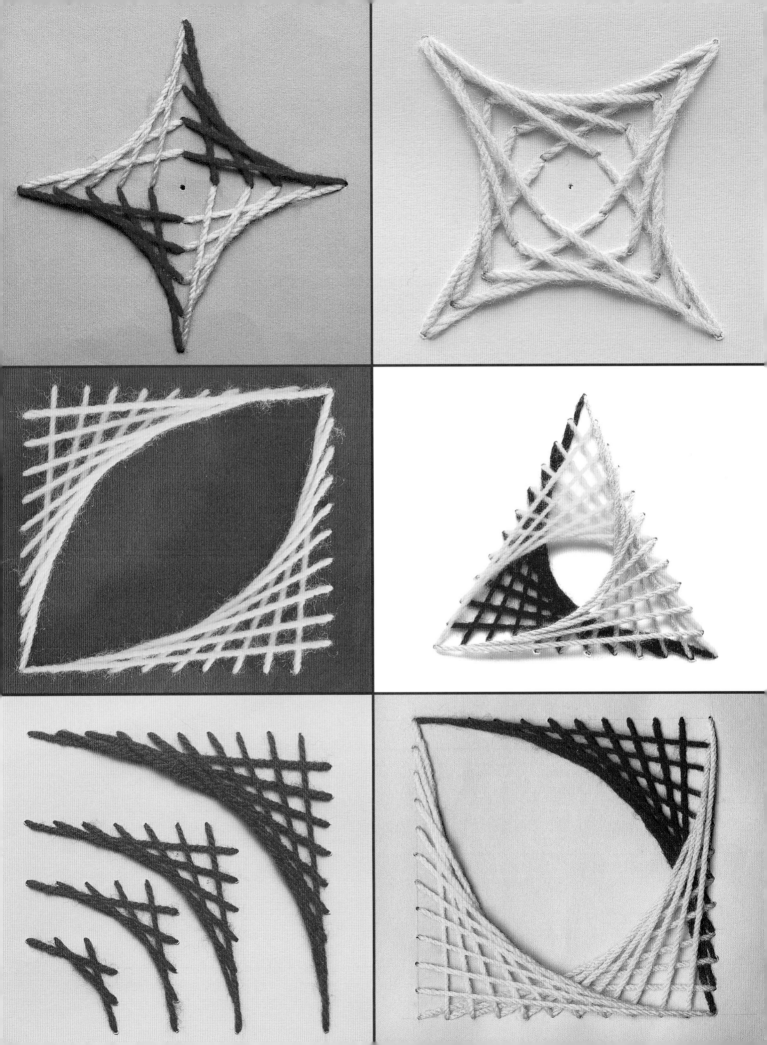

Weaving kit

YARN

YARN AND
DARNING
NEEDLE

THICK PAPER OR
POSTERBOARD

SCISSORS

PENCIL

RULER

SQUARE

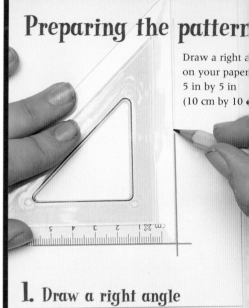

Preparing the pattern

Draw a right a
on your paper
5 in by 5 in
(10 cm by 10

1. Draw a right angle

Weaving tips

• Use thick paper or posterboard.
If the paper is too thin it will rip
when you pull the thread through.
• For large patterns use yarn, but
for smaller designs you could use
lighter thread.
• When you get the hang of it, try
using different-colored pieces of
yarn. When you are really good,
try different patterns.
• The most important thing is to
EXPERIMENT and HAVE FUN.

Try the diamond design

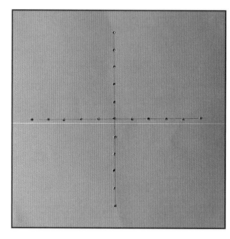

Start

The more holes you make, the bigger the pattern will be...

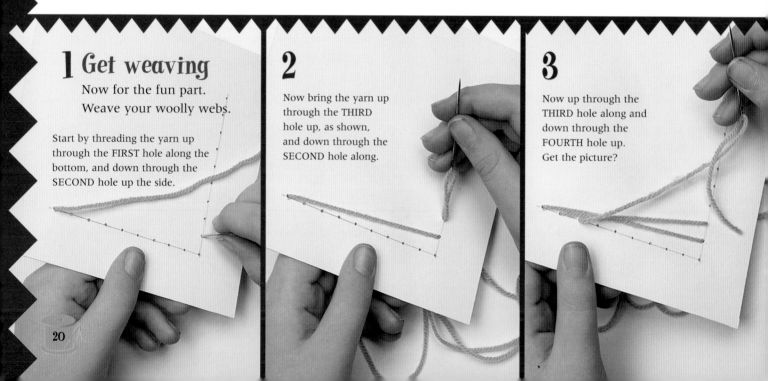

1 Get weaving

Now for the fun part.
Weave your woolly webs.

Start by threading the yarn up
through the FIRST hole along the
bottom, and down through the
SECOND hole up the side.

2

Now bring the yarn up
through the THIRD
hole up, as shown,
and down through the
SECOND hole along.

3

Now up through the
THIRD hole along and
down through the
FOURTH hole up.
Get the picture?

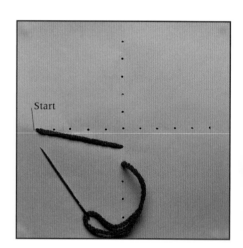

20

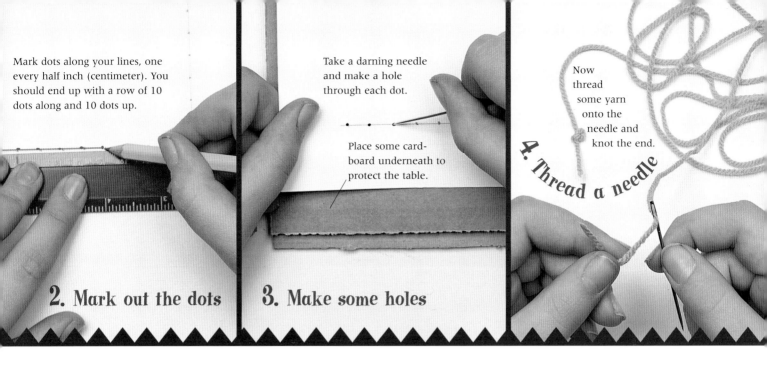

Mark dots along your lines, one every half inch (centimeter). You should end up with a row of 10 dots along and 10 dots up.

2. Mark out the dots

Take a darning needle and make a hole through each dot.

Place some cardboard underneath to protect the table.

3. Make some holes

Now thread some yarn onto the needle and knot the end.

4. Thread a needle

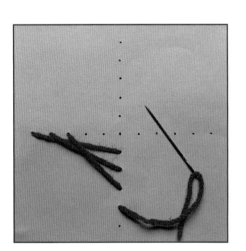
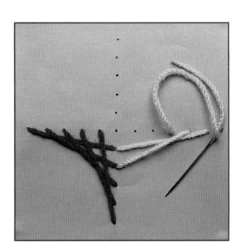
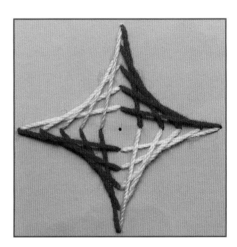

and remember, you can use each hole more than once—go on, weave a giant web!

4

Keep weaving in this pattern until you have no more holes to fill.

5

The last hole you use should be the top one, so thread down through it and stop.

6

Turn the paper over, tie a knot as close to the stitch as possible, and cut off the yarn end.

Get weaving

wonderful webs in rainbow colors.

Paper plate

yarn

A paper plate and scraps of yarn create a rainbow web to brighten up your day.

To weave a web
you will need
- A paper plate or posterboard d
- Scraps of yarn
- Darning needle

1

Draw out a zig-zag edge around the plate and cut out the triangles.

2

See page 7 for other ways to start off.

knot

Loop the yarn around two opposite spikes, making sure they cross in the middle, and tie a kot in the center.

3

Keep crossing the yarn from spike to spike, making sure the yarn crosses through the middle.

The yarn will go around this one next.

4

Keep going backward and forward across the plate.

5

Turn your plate over and it should look like this. Tie the end of the yarn into a knot.

6

Thread a piece of yarn onto a needle. From the middle, weave the needle between the strands.

It will look strange at first, but after about six rows, it will even out.

7

As you weave, make sure you pull the yarn tight into the middle

8

Knot a new piece of yarn to the last one and just keep on weaving.

use up your old scraps

Continue weaving in different colors until there's no more room.

23

Keep on weaving

Looms are frames used for weaving fabric. Make a simple loom and try creating a piece of fabric—and then start to weave anything you can find!

Homemade loom

A shoebox lid is ideal. Cut the same number of slits on opposite ends, then thread yarn backward and forward.

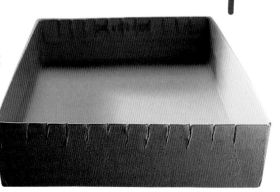

1

⭐ **Ask an adult** to cut the slits—they may need to use a sharp knife.

2

Wrap the yarn around the first slit to hold it in place.

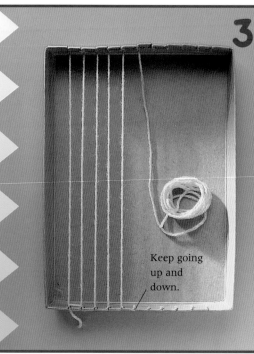

3

Keep going up and down.

4

Thread the yarn above and below the main strands and forward and back.

5

Now try weaving other things that you can find.

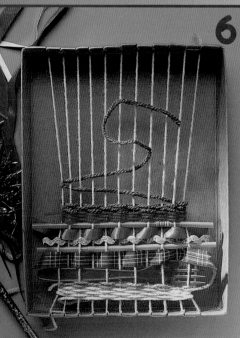

6

Weave and weave until you reach the top.

A work of weaving art—hang it on the wall for all to see.

Ribbon

Yarn

Plastic
Knife

Pencil

Tinsel

Straw

Fancy
Ribbon

Plastic
Fork

why not make a friendship bracelet for your favorite friend?

Knitting

Master the skill of knitting. Begin with your fingers and thumbs and work up to needles. As well as yarn, you will need lots of patience, so DON'T give up.

Finger knitting

This is also called finger crochet. Wind the yarn around your thumb twice, then pick up the first loop and take it over the second. Keep repeating this until it has grown to the length you want.

1 Wind the yarn around your thumb twice.

2 Pick up the first loop.

3 Take it over the second loop.

It's growing

4 Keep going.

5 Carefully pull the yarn.

6 Pull the yarn so the stitch is secure on your finger.

7 Repeat the steps. The first loop is there, so wind the yarn to make the second.

Use two pieces of different-colored yarn to make a multicolored wristband.

As you repeat the steps, the bracelet will grow and grow.

Knit a blanket

Once you have the hang of finger knitting, you will have a good idea how to cast on to needles and start knitting. Using plain stitch, you can make a finger puppet from a single square, and if you get really ambitious, you can make lots of squares to make a blanket.

I'm in stitches!

Knitted pals

Ted sits and knits

a pal or two to play with, complete with cozy hats.

Knitted hat

Easy knitting

Knitting is surprisingly simple, and once you get the hang of it, you can knit anything you want. All the knitted projects in this book are made only from knitted squares and rectangles—this makes them really easy! Start off with Ted, move on to his pals, then knit them all warm scarves and hats.

Off we go...

How to get started

You will need...

Casting on
This is how you get the stitches onto the needle. The pattern will tell you how many to cast on.

Tie the yarn to the needle, then pick up the yarn and twist it once.	Now twist the same piece again.	Slip the loop onto the needle.	Pull the yarn so that the stitch is quite tight.

Knitting stitches
Follow these instructions and just keep knitting and knitting and knitting!

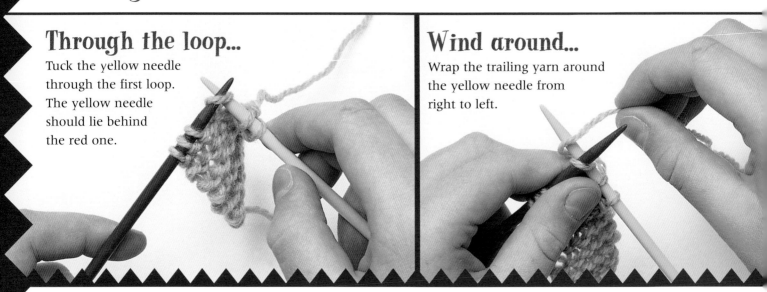

Through the loop...
Tuck the yellow needle through the first loop. The yellow needle should lie behind the red one.

Wind around...
Wrap the trailing yarn around the yellow needle from right to left.

Casting off
When you have have knitted enough rows, finish it by off by "casting off."

Knit two stitches as normal

On the yellow needle, take hold of the first stitch.

Pull the stitch right over the second and off the needle.

Knit another stitch a do the same again.

SCISSORS

BALL OF YARN

Row counter

This is a handy gadget that slides onto a needle. Each time you do a row, turn the the dial to show the number of rows you have done.

ROW COUNTER

Now you've made a stitch.

Repeat these steps for as many stitches as you need.

Now begin your first row of knitting.

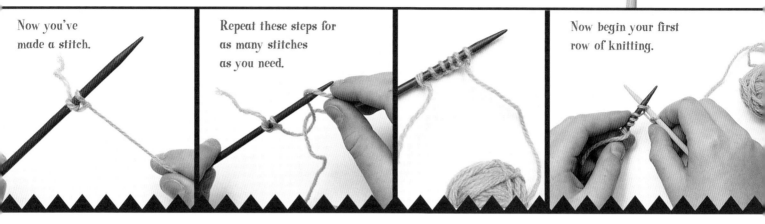

Under it goes...

Bring the yellow needle back up to the front with the loop still attached.

Off it comes

Release the stitch off the red needle, keeping it on the yellow one.

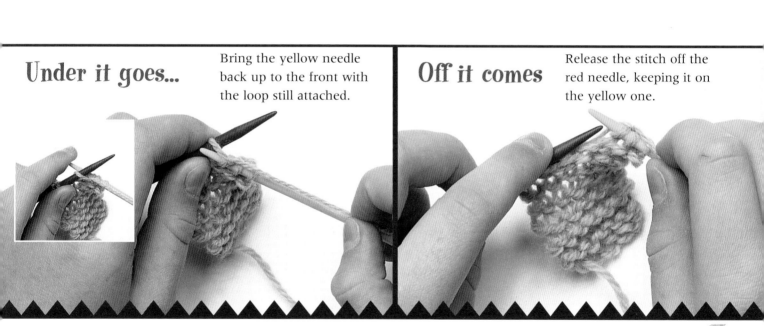

Keep going until you have one stitch left.

Snip the yarn.

Bring the end of the yarn through the loop and pull tight. This will secure it.

Watch me jump

Making Ted
Knit five pieces, sew them up, stuff them, and put them together. Hello, Ted

1

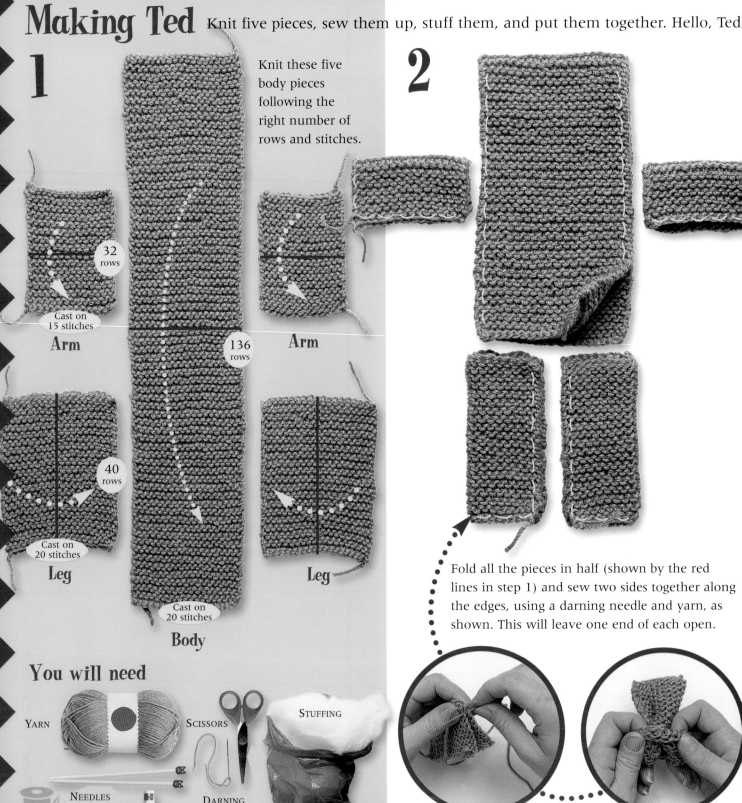

Knit these five body pieces following the right number of rows and stitches.

Arm
32 rows
Cast on 15 stitches

Arm

Body
136 rows
Cast on 20 stitches

Leg
40 rows
Cast on 20 stitches

Leg

2

Fold all the pieces in half (shown by the red lines in step 1) and sew two sides together along the edges, using a darning needle and yarn, as shown. This will leave one end of each open.

You will need

YARN

SCISSORS

STUFFING

NEEDLES

ROW COUNTER

DARNING NEEDLE

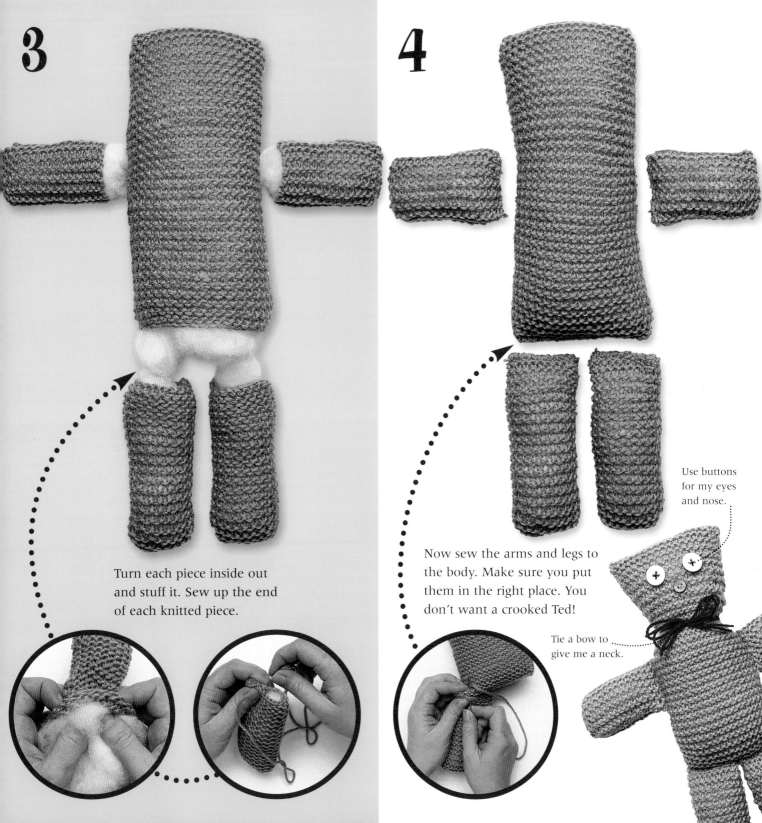

3

Turn each piece inside out and stuff it. Sew up the end of each knitted piece.

4

Now sew the arms and legs to the body. Make sure you put them in the right place. You don't want a crooked Ted!

Use buttons for my eyes and nose.

Tie a bow to give me a neck.

Ted's friends

You can't just make Ted, you need to make Ted's friends, too. And what happens if they get cold? Knit them scarves and hats, of course!

Make a friend for Ted

Ted's friend is very simple because he has wobbly legs.

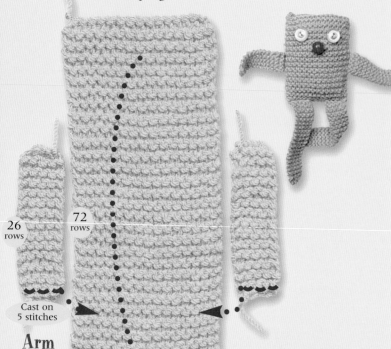

26 rows

72 rows

Cast on 5 stitches

Arm

Body

Cast on 16 stitches

40 rows

Leg

Cast on 5 stitches

Making friends

Knit the five body pieces following the rows and stitches as shown. Fold the body in half, sew up two sides, turn it inside out, and stuff it—just like Ted on page 32. Then sew the body up and simply attach the arms and legs.

Beanie hats

Everyone needs a hat.

Hat-making

Ted's friend wants a
Cast on 54 stitches
and knit 20 rows. Fo
it in half, as above, a
sew the top and side
together. Put it on a
turn up the bottom.

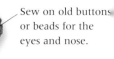

Sew on old buttons
or beads for the
eyes and nose.

34

A pom-pon for the hat

Cut out two discs from posterboard. Cut a hole in the middle of each.

2 in (5 cm) across

Put the discs together and tie a piece of yarn around them.

Use different colors.

Wind the yarn around and around through the middle and over the top. Stop when the discs are covered.

Put a pair of scissors between the discs and snip the yarn all around.

Tie a piece of yarn tightly around the pom-pon.

Take away the discs and fluff it up!

A fringe for the scarf

Knit Ted's long scarf as shown and finish if off nicely with a fringe.

Double up a piece of yarn and bring it up through the hole.

Stick a needle through the scarf above the first row.

Take the two ends, bring them up through the loop, and pull downward for the fringe. Repeat along the row.

140 rows

Cast on 12 stitches

Ted's hat

Ted's cozy hat is made by casting on 66 stitches and knitting 46 rows. Turn it up and finish it off with a bright pom-pon. Once you can make Ted's scarf and hat, why not try making full-size ones for friends? They make great gifts.

String things

All wound up! From see-through string balls and fluffy pom-pons, there's a whole new woolly world to discover.

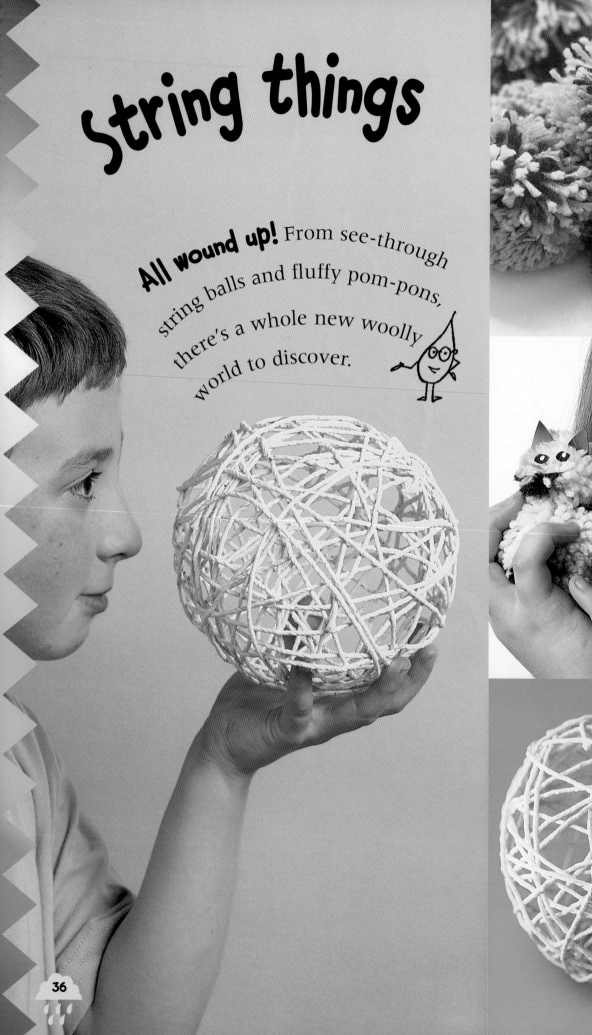

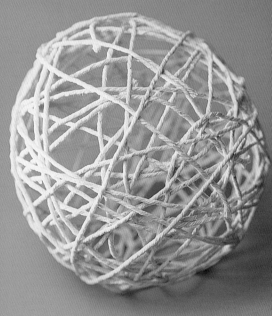

Juggle those pom-pons!

How to make a string thing

You will need • Balloon • String or yarn • Wallpaper paste • Vaseline

Blow up a balloon and spread Vaseline all over it to keep the string from sticking to the balloon.

Mix up a bowl of wallpaper paste.

Cut some pieces of string, about 22 in (60 cm) long.

Dip the string into the paste, then wrap it around the balloon.

Add more and more and more string until you have enough.

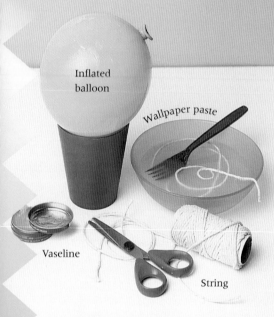

Inflated balloon

Wallpaper paste

Vaseline

String

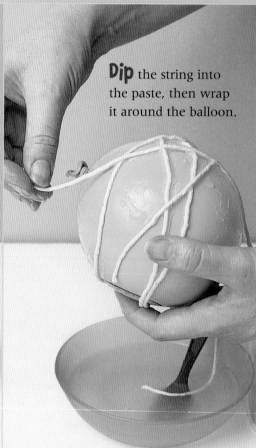

Watch out!
This part gets messy

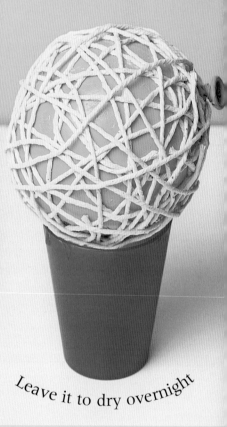

Leave it to dry overnight

How to make a pom-pon

You will need • Thin cardboard • Yarn

Tip: The larger the disks, the bigger your pom-pon will turn out.

Knot the yarn in place.

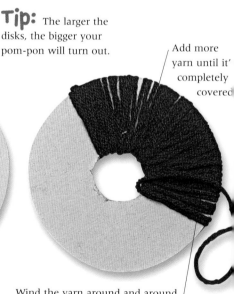

Add more yarn until it's completely covered

4 in (10 cm)

Cut out two cardboard disks.

Cut a 1-in (2.5-cm) hole in the middle of each disk.

Put the two disks together.

Wind the yarn around and around, through the middle and over the top.

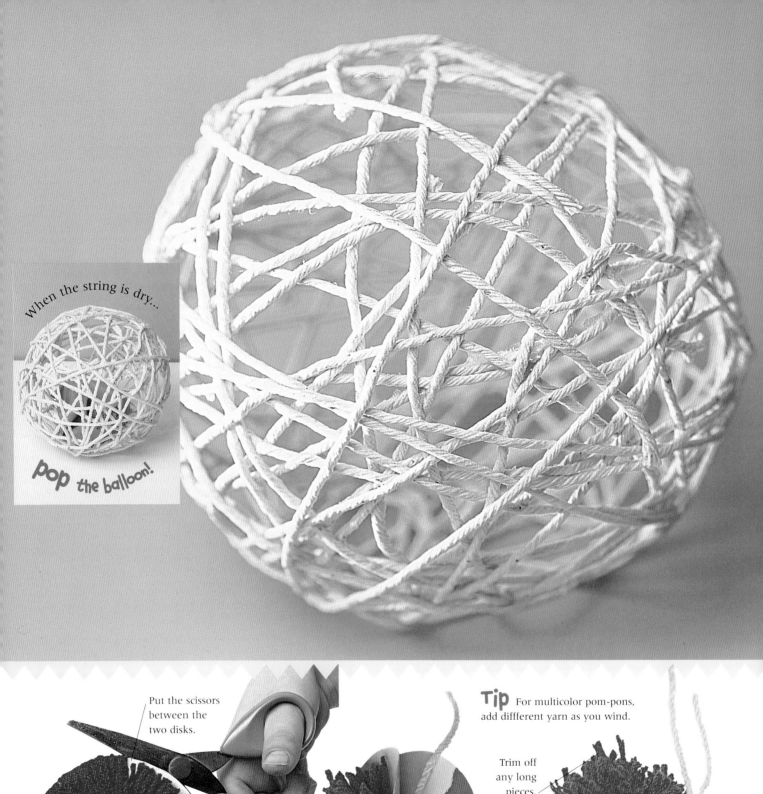

When the string is dry...

pop the balloon!

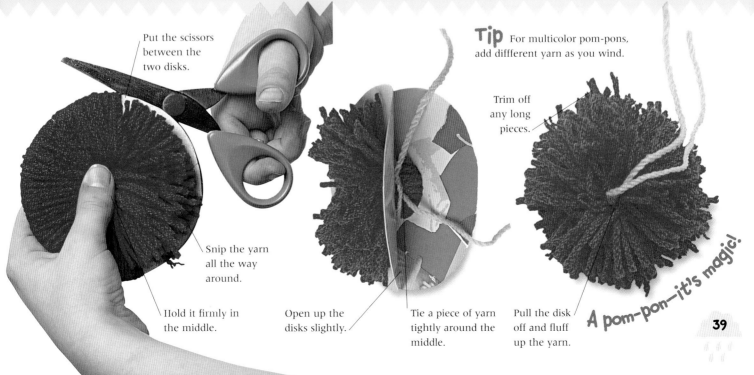

Put the scissors between the two disks.

Snip the yarn all the way around.

Hold it firmly in the middle.

Open up the disks slightly.

Tie a piece of yarn tightly around the middle.

Tip For multicolor pom-pons, add diffferent yarn as you wind.

Trim off any long pieces.

Pull the disk off and fluff up the yarn.

A pom-pon—it's magic!

39

Sun clock

Time to watch the clock in the yard.

what time is it?

Impress your friends by being able to tell the time without looking at a watch. How do you do it? By using the sun.

How to make a clock

You will need:

- Paper plate
- Terracotta plant pot
- Stick or garden cane
- Watch
- Strips of paper
- Sticky tack

Before you assemble your sun clock, decorate the plate, stick, and pot.

1. Make a hole in the center of the plate and push the cane through.

Put sticky tack around the hole.

2. Now put the cane through the hole in the plant pot.

Press the plate onto the sticky tack.

3. Make sure the plate doesn't turn easily on the stick.

use the sunlight to set your clock

You will need a whole sunny day to set your clock so that you can read it the next day.

1. Place your clock in a sunny area.

2. The stick will cast a shadow across the plate. This is the sun telling you the time.

10 o'clock　　12 o'clock　　2 o'clock

3. Now look at your watch, and mark the shadow on each hour with a strip of paper. For example, at 10 o'clock mark the shadow, then continue until the sun goes down.

4. The next day, tell the time by seeing where the shadow falls!

It's just past 3 o'clock

Noon 12
11
10
9
8
1
2
3
4
5
6
7

Make the 12 o'clock strip look different to remind you where it is.

41

Sun catchers

Shimmering, glittering mobiles

twist and turn in the breeze, catching the bright sunlight.

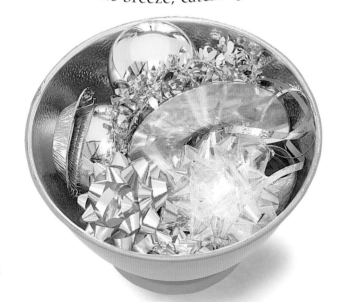

Silver scraps

Look out for things lying around the house that reflect the sun. Try old CDs, gift wrap, and shiny plastic bottles.

How to catch the sun

Jazz up your backyard by finding anything that shines, glitters, or shimmers, and make mobiles with it. As they twist and turn in the sunlight, they glisten and dance. And on a cloudy day, they will still cheer up the yard.

Spiral catcher

The basic shape of this sun-catcher is the spiral of aluminum foil and a used CD. But with a bit of imagination, you can turn it into a real dazzler. Add sequins, shiny buttons, old Christmas decorations, or even double up the spiral and make an enormous spiral catcher!

String

Twisted foil

CD

1. Cut about 2 ft (60 cm) of aluminum foil.

2. Scrunch and twist it up in your hands until it is a solid tube.

3. Twist it around your hand. Add another for a longer spiral.

4. Tie a piece of string to the top of the spiral, then tie the other end around a CD.

Leave some extra string at the top to hang it up.

Decide where you want the CD to hang before you tie it.

Dancing paper plates

The secret to the paper plate catcher is to decorate both sides of the plate—that way, whichever way it turns, it will sparkle.

1. Draw a zigzag around a paper plate and cut it out.

Shiny candy wrappers

2. Now cover it with lots of shiny things.

Foil dish

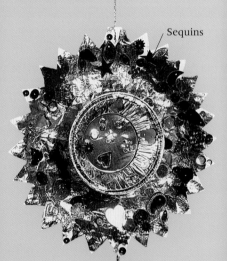

Sequins

3. Tape some string to the back and add any other shiny things you can find.

Christmas ornament

44

Bottle-bell mobile

• Take some string and attach a round piece of posterboard, 1 in (3 cm) across, halfway along it by poking a hole through the card.

• Thread a button below it.

• Attach shiny decorations such as CDs, ornaments, and anything else that shimmers.

• Now simply thread the bottle-bell through the top of the string and it will sit on the posterboard.

How to make the bottle-bell

1. Cut off the bottom of a soda bottle.

2. Cut ¹/2-in (2-cm) strips about two-thirds of the way up the bottle.

3. Roll each strip up with your fingers and they will curl.

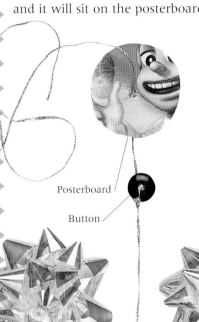

These old, shiny gift bows are perfect. Squeeze two together and they will stay attached!

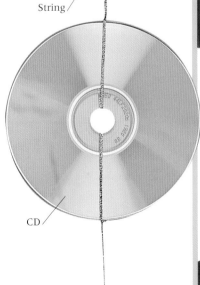

Posterboard

Button

String

CD

Ornament

Let's sparkle in the sunlight

Thread the bottle-bell along the string until it sits on the posterboard.

4. Thread the string through the neck of the bottle.

45

Carry around good herb smells

What's the Sense?

Some sensible ways

to make the most of your senses.

Look at all the plant colors and shapes

Silver, purple, orange, green

Feathery, wispy, furry, wrinkly

These plant labels are made from Ping-Pong balls on sticks.

Sight

Look out

Decorate your garden with painted pots and plant labels to show what's growing where. See page 169.

Keep an eye on the garden

Touchy-feely

The more you touch herbs, the more they give off their aroma. Rub the plants between your fingers and smell them.

Soft and furry

Touch

46

Good taste

Herbs can help make food taste even better. Chop up the leaves or use them whole.

Taste

Mix together chopped chives and sour cream.

Mint

Coriander

Thyme

Rosemary

Parsley

Sage

Try it with a baked potato.

A bunch of herb leaves can be added to soups and stews while they are cooking to add extra taste.

Stop! Listen!

Stop for a moment. Stay very still. What do you hear? Are there birds singing, bees buzzing, or leaves rustling? Enjoy the sounds your garden makes.

Smell

Smelly bundles

Tie up some herbs in a bundle and pop them in a drawer or even your pocket. Lavender is great to use, since it has a lovely, strong smell.

Catnip sock toy

Cats go wild over catnip.

Fresh herbs all wrapped up.

Freshen up the dog's basket

Listen to the wind
with a wind chime

Sound

47

How to Come to Your Senses

Find out what to use your herbs for, and start your very own herb garden.

Plant pot wind chime

Terra-cotta pots are the best things for creating a soothing jingle-jangle in your windy garden.

TERRA-COTTA POT STRING PLASTIC LID BEADS, ETC.

Tie the string to a branch in the garden.

Knot the strings together.

Leave part of the string hanging down below the pot.

Pull some string through the hole in the pot. Attach a bead to the end that will sit under the hole.

Tie the four pieces of string to the main piece.

Ask an adult to help you cut a large hole in the center of the plastic lid, then eight smaller ones around the edge. Tie a piece of string to every other hole.

Attach a length of string to each hole and hang a pebble, shell, or bead from each one.

Tie a pebble to the string hanging through the center, to weigh it down.

Self-contained herb garden

Spring and summertime

Conjure up an instant herb garden in a pot. Choose herbs for their smell, color, or taste. Decorate the container with a design that suits your pot garden.

Keep it watered and in a warm, sheltered spot.

These are small plants. After a year they may need to move to a bigger pot.

Parsley

Lemon balm

Sage

Oregano

Dill

Find a pot large enough to take three to five plants.

Layer of pebbles

48

Handy herbs

They may be small, but herbs have the most amazing number of different uses. From food flavorings and scents to dyes and healing remedies, herbs are essential to our lives.

Refreshing mints

There are more flavors of mint than you could ever imagine—peppermint, spearmint, and lemon mint, to name a few. Mint herbs are used in many things, such as chewing gum, toothpaste, and flavored teas. Can you think of any more?

Sweet smells

Herbs such as lavender and camomile have a lovely strong smell. These are great herbs for your herb bags or simply to put in a drawer to make clothes smell nice.

Savory tastes

Rosemary, thyme, parsley, sage, and oregano are herbs that are most commonly used to enhance savory foods, such as sausages, fish, or vegetables. They all have very different tastes.

Cat's best friend

Catnip is simply irresistible to cats. Fill a bag with catnip and watch your kitty go crazy!

Catnip sock

Create a face on a colorful sock with buttons and beads, and fill the sock with catnip. Add rice or dried peas to make it heavier. Tie a knot and let your cat loose on it.

Dried catnip

Herb wristband

Place some fresh herbs in a scarf, roll it up, and tie it into a knot. Take the lovely smells with you.

Try some rosemary, lavender, or mint.

Fold the scarf, roll it up, and tie it in a knot.

Wear it on your wrist

Smelly bundles

The smell of lavender helps you sleep and also makes a room smell nice. Try making your own herb pouch. Place some lavender in a scarf, tie it up with an elastic band, and add a ribbon for decoration.

Fresh herb bundle

Elastic band

Lavender bundle

Fill the pot half-way with compost.

Take the plants out of their small pots, position them, then fill up the gaps with compost.

Remember to water them

49

Paper roses

Fill a vase with home-grown tissue flowers and give a bunch to your mom.

Wild roses

Create a really wild, colorful bunch by mixing and matching the colors. If you want to make rose trees, see page 165 for instructions.

To make a rose

Take a piece of tissue paper and a plate about 6 in (15 cm) wide.

Draw around the plate and cut out six discs the same size.

Six tissue paper discs.

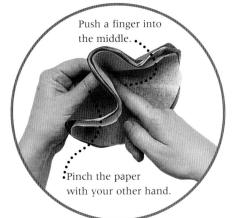

Push a finger into the middle.

Pinch the paper with your other hand.

Squeeze the bottom of the paper tightly.

Tape the paper to a straw.

Rose trees

Rows of roses

SMALL PLATE

TISSUE PAPER

TAPE

PEN

SCISSORS

DRINKING STRAWS

Perfect petals

Finally, pull the layers apart carefully to fluff up the flower.

Salt dough

Four activities in one

1. Mixing
2. Modeling
3. Cooking
4. Painting

Mix the dough and squeeze it into any shape you like, for hours of doughy fun.

To make the dough

You will need

water
1 cup
(200 ml)

Salt
1 cup (300 g)

Flour
3 cups
(300 g)

Oil
2 tsp

Put all of the ingredients into a bowl.

Squeeze the mixture together.

Pat it into a ball.

Roll it out

Now have fun!

Make a good impression

Play with your dough

Roll it, rake it, squash it, squeeze it. Look around your house for objects to press into the dough. You can create all kinds of effects and shapes, and if you don't like them, roll them up and start over.

If the dough gets sticky, sprinkle on some flour.

Bear necessities

Make the bear shapes.

Stick them together.

Squash a paperclip onto the back.

Bake the bear, then paint it.

Tie on a ribbon.

Baking your shapes

Place your shapes on a baking tray.

If the shapes are big, they will take longer to cook, and if they are delicate, they may break more easily, so keep them small and chunky.

Let them cool down before you paint them.

⭐ **Ask an adult** to help with the oven.

Bake for 20 minutes at 350°F (180°C)

Painting and decorating

When the baked dough has cooled down, you can paint it with poster or acrylic paint. Try mixing a little PVA glue to the paint (about 1 part PVA to 2 parts paint)— this will make it tough and shiny.

More about PVA glue on page 7.

Keeping your dough

You can save your unbaked dough by covering it in plastic wrap. It will keep for about two weeks.

Save it for a rainy day

55

Fun and Games

Come and play

Scrap bags
We're full of beans!

57

Throw together a scrap bag

Here, catch!

To make a bag

Use the scrap bag pattern to measure the size of your bag. Cut out a piece of fabric and fold it in half.

Fold it in half.

LEAVE A HOLE

STITCHING LINE

Scrap bag pattern
Follow this
pattern to help
you with the size.

FOLD THE FABRIC HERE

STITCHING LINE

LEAVE A HOLE

Leave an opening at the top.

Back stitch around the open sides.

Turn the bag inside out.

Fill it with dried peas or beans.

To finish it off, stitch up the hole at the top.

Pin it together

Sew up the sides

Turn inside out and fill up

Close it up

Back stitch

A good stitch to use is back stitch, because it completely seals the sides. Don't be fooled into thinking you can do a simple running stitch—if you do, the beans will fall out!

See page 5 for back stitch instructions.

Sew or use PVA glue to stick on the faces.

Scrap bag games

Target practice

Set up a target area around a bucket and challenge your family to score high. Make up the rules yourself!

Juggling

Start with two, then build up your bags. A perfect practice for a rainy day.

Play catch

Throw a bag for a friend to catch. If they miss, they go down on one knee; miss again, they go down on two knees; and so on, until they are lying down.

Bad luck! To score 100, it has to go right into the bowl.

100

50

25

Good shot! that's 100 points!

59

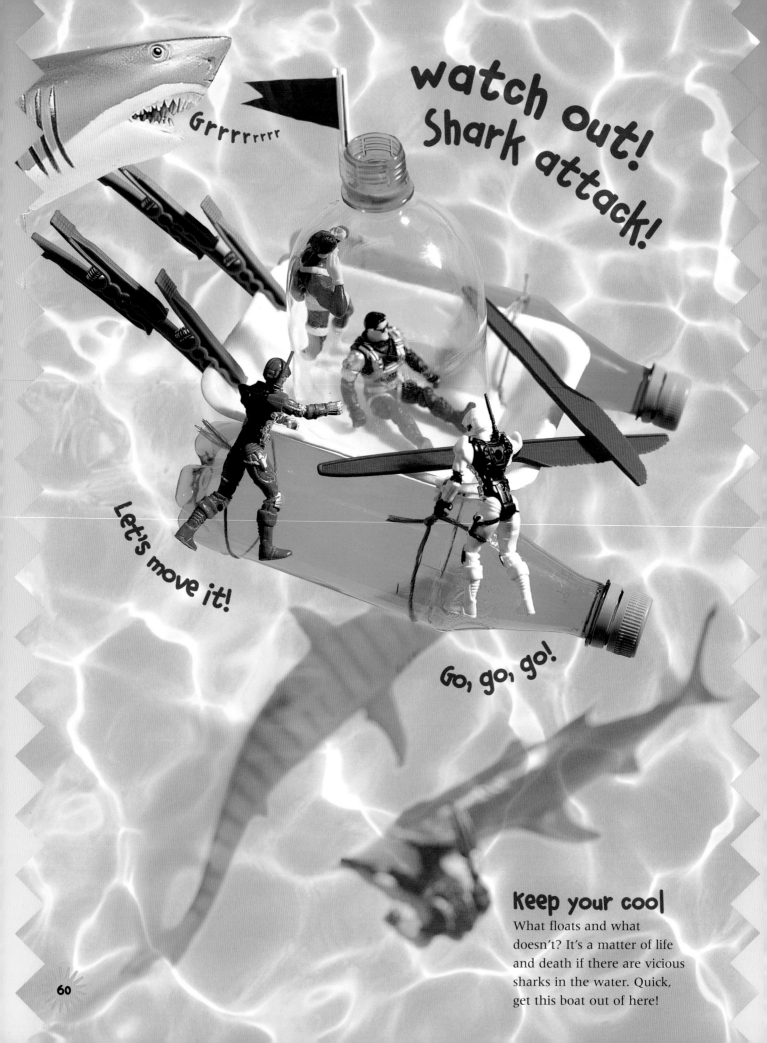

watch out!
Shark attack!

Grrrrrrrr

Let's move it!

Go, go, go!

keep your cool

What floats and what
doesn't? It's a matter of life
and death if there are vicious
sharks in the water. Quick,
get this boat out of here!

Crafty boats

Think or you'll sink! All you need to remember is, if it floats it'll make a boat. You'll need it to float if the sharks are around!

use anything you can find that floats for boat-building materials

To make a basic boat

All you need are two plastic bottles and a plastic food tray. When you are finished, add special features, such as a control deck or a racing spoiler.

Carefully make a hole in each corner.

Plastic bottle   Plastic food tray   Plastic bottle

Scissors and string

Tie a piece of string through each hole and tightly around each bottle.

★ **Ask an adult** to help when you are near water.

61

Tiny camps for tiny toys

Here's a tiny adventure world—
a mini camp. Let's get building!

This way to the building site

Portable campsite
Camps on trays are very useful because you can take them inside if it rains. You could use anything to decorate your landscape—you could even add a little soil and plant some small flowers in it. Work out what you would like best in a campsite and get building!

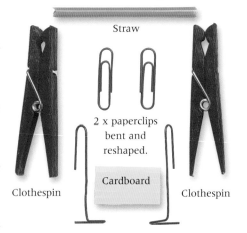

Twig frame tent
Gather up some small twigs, make the frame, and hang a piece of material over it.

Tie tightly with string.

For the legs, tie three twigs together at the top.

Stand the two ends up and place another twig across them for the tent frame.

Tiny Swing

Straw

2 x paperclips bent and reshaped.

Cardboard

Clothespin   Clothespin

Tape the paperclips to the cardboard to make a seat. Then hook them over the straw.

Baby bunting
Find some pieces of colored paper and a long piece of string.

Cut the paper into diamond shapes.

Glue one side of the diamond.

Fold it over the string with the glue on the inside to form a triangle.

Get camping!

Put it together! Take a tray and fill it will sand, gravel, or soil. Find some pebbles or rocks and place them around the edge. Now use your imagination to fill it with teeny, tiny camping gear.

I can't wait to move in

Pebbles create a good landscape.

Use pebbles to keep the material down

A tiny picnic stand made with three twigs and a bottle top.

Sponge fish

A pond made out of a food container.

You could use sand as your base

65

Box rooms where your toys can live. Decorate and furnish them with odds and ends

Find a cardboard box

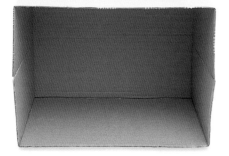

Measure the paper

Use wrapping paper or paint your own wallpaper.

Draw and cut out windows

you will need

For the house itself:
- A cardboard box
- Scissors, ruler, and pen
- Decorated wallpaper
- Material for the carpet
- Glue

⭐ **Ask an adult** to help cut the thick card.

Decorate the walls

Glue the wallpaper to the inside of the box.

Cover the floor

A washcloth makes a very good carpet.

Ahh, home, sweet home

Come in out of the rain

All I need now is a comfy chair

How to make scrap furniture

Collect boxes, cartons, and other bits and pieces that are going to be thrown away—imagine how many you will gather over the weeks for those rainy days. You'll have a great collection.

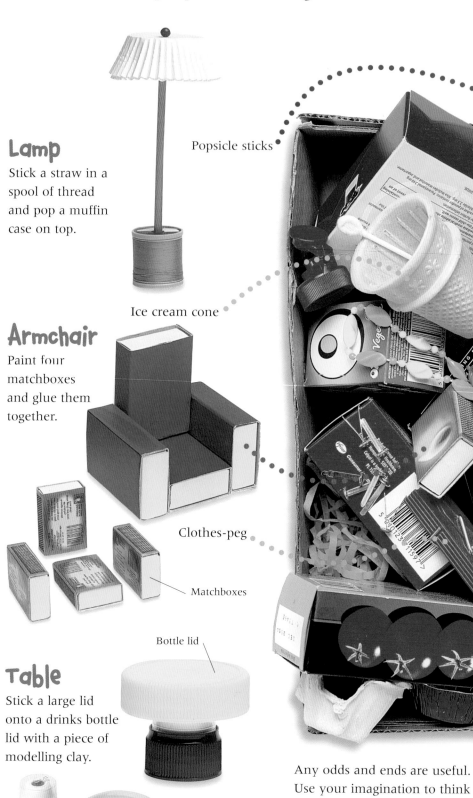

Lamp
Stick a straw in a spool of thread and pop a muffin case on top.

Popsicle sticks

Ice cream cone

Armchair
Paint four matchboxes and glue them together.

Clothes-peg

Matchboxes

Small boxes

Create a cupboard from a small box. Cut out a door and attach a split pin handle onto it.

Bottle lid

Table
Stick a large lid onto a drinks bottle lid with a piece of modelling clay.

Modelling clay

Any odds and ends are useful. Use your imagination to think of other bits of furniture that can go inside your box room.

You will need

- Odds and ends from around the house.
- Adhesive tape
- Paper fasteners
- Paint and brushes
- Modelling clay
- Paper fasteners
- Glue

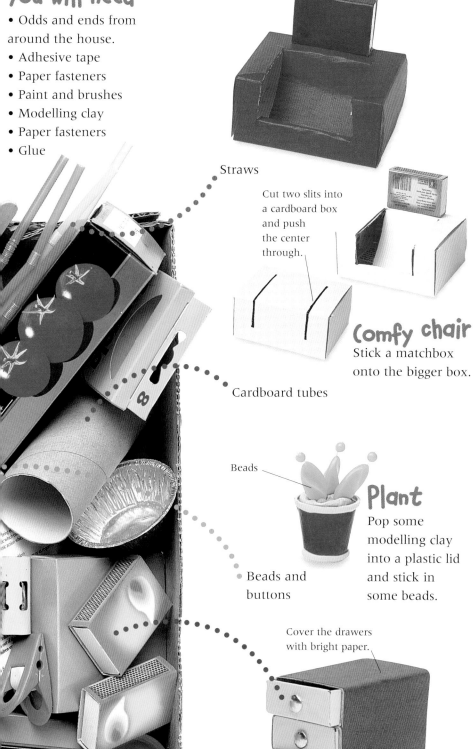

Straws

Cut two slits into a cardboard box and push the center through.

Comfy chair
Stick a matchbox onto the bigger box.

Cardboard tubes

Beads

Plant
Pop some modelling clay into a plastic lid and stick in some beads.

Beads and buttons

Cover the drawers with bright paper.

Paper fastener

Drawers
Three matchboxes and paper fasteners.

Plastic spoon

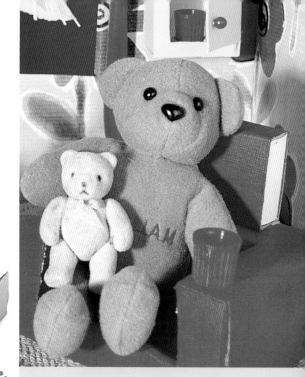

Lids and caps

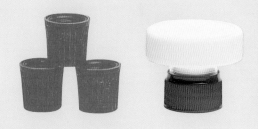

Lids from empty tubes of paint make tiny cups or plant pots. Lids and caps can be made into tiny tables.

Bag of Tricks

This bag is not what it seems— it has the power to transform anything that enters it.

In go some handkerchiefs one by one...

Abracadabra!

Hey Presto! Out they come...

...all knotted

What goes in doesn't always come out...

That's magic!

Quick, hide your valuables or they'll disappear!

How to Make your Bewitched Bag

Grab the limelight using the amazing enchanted bag. All you need is the bag, two sets of identical, brightly colored handkerchiefs, and lots of practice.

Glue together three pieces of fabric, each about 10 x 8 in (25 x 20 cm) in size, leaving the top open.

Glue the material

What's the Bag's Secret?

Secret pocket

Front pocket

This quirky bag is actually not just one bag but two. It has two pockets, so that you can put the single handkerchiefs in one part while the knotted ones will already be in the other part ready for you to produce at the end.

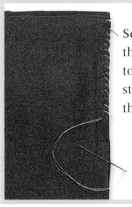

Sew the three sides together to strengthen the bag.

Preparing your Trick

Knot together one set of handkerchiefs and place them in a pocket. Then fold down the top of the bag so that the empty pocket is open for the audience to feel inside it. Practice folding down the top—you will see that you can expose the pockets one at a time. When you have mastered it, try putting other things into the bag as well.

Sew up the edges

Decorate the front

In go three shiny cars ...out they come on the socks!

Performing the Trick

Explain to the audience that you have an empty bag. Let them see and feel inside it. Yes, it's empty. Now, with a dramatic flourish, put the handerkerchiefs into the bag one at a time.

Fold over the top, revealing the empty pocket

1 I'm putting the hankies in one by one

2 Now I turn up the sides of the bag

3 Abracadabra!

4 I fold over the top of the bag to reveal the secret pocket

5 Swishhh! Wow! A trail of handkerchiefs, all tied up!

The Vanishing Coin

Who can lend me a coin? Assure the audience that they will see the money again as you make it disappear before their eyes. It's OK—you can make it reappear!

Cylinder

See-through cup

Coin

Performing mat

Show the coin 1

Cover the cup 2

Bring it Back

Now that the coin has gone, get it back. Mutter a few magic words, put the cylinder back on the cup, lift it up—and hey presto, the coin is back! Put the cylinder down, release it from the cup, and you have the same layout you had at the start. Give the coin back to the amazed owner.

74

Place the cylinder back over the cup and lift it up.

Don't let the cup slip out.

Phew it's back!

Prepare the Props

It is very important that your props all do their jobs well—they must be made very carefully. The performing mat and the cup base should be made from the same paper, the cup base must be attached neatly, and the cylinder should exactly cover the cup—no bigger or smaller.

Performing mat

Be sure to make the mat big enough for the trick.

Draw around the cup and cut the disc out.

Cup base

Glue the paper disc to the rim of the cup.

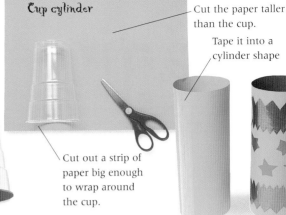

Cup cylinder

Cut the paper taller than the cup.

Tape it into a cylinder shape

Cut out a strip of paper big enough to wrap around the cup.

Decorate the cylinder.

Conceal the coin 3

Take off the cylinder It's GONE! 4

Performing the Trick

★ The key to this trick is that the base of the cup is covered with the same color paper as the mat you perform your trick on.

★ Show everyone the cylinder and coin—but don't let anyone see the base of the cup. Then, follow the steps above to cover it all up.

★ Remember, the coin will always be under the cup but beneath the paper—so don't lift the cup up at all until you want to bring it back.

I can't believe my eyes

Where did my coin go?

Magic Folder

Slip a note into the magic folder and watch it evaporate into thin air by simply closing the folder up and opening it again. Impossible!

Watch in wonder as things come and go from the magic folder

In it goes

Slip the object inside the envelope

1

Bring it back

Fold the envelope up again

4

Close it **2**

Open it up again
The object has gone!

Empty **3**

Close up the folder **5**

Open it up and it's back!

Astonishing! **6**

How to Make the Magic Folder

This folder is magical because it is back to front and front to back at the same time—whichever way you turn it.

Take two identical envelopes.

Place one, with the opening facing down, underneath the ribbon.

Get two identical envelopes

Cut two pieces of thick construction paper or cardboard, 8 x 6 in (21 x 15 cm).

Cut three 7¹/₂ in (19 cm) ribbons or strips of paper.

Cut the cardboard and ribbons

Glue the other envelope, with the opening facing up, exactly over the other one.

Stick them under and over the ribbon

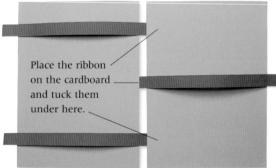

Place the ribbon on the cardboard and tuck them under here.

Place the ribbon on the cardboard

Glue some colored paper to the outside of the folder.

Cover up the outside

The ends on the outside fold over the edge.

Glue the little strips of ribbon that you can see with strong glue.

The ends on the inside remain flat.

Turn over the card. This will be the outside of the folder.

Glue the ribbons in position

Make a design for both sides of the outside of the folder, but make sure that they are exactly the same.

Decorate both sides the same

1 Follow this sequence

Try it out

Practice opening and closing the folder both ways. It's amazing, isn't it? Once you have figured out how it works, you're ready to try it out.

2 Open it up and slip in a star

The Secret?

The secret is that the folder is double-sided. The way the ribbons are attached makes it possible for you to open it two ways. Because of the way you have placed the envelopes, each has its own opening. So when you do the trick:

* Fill the envelope
* Close the folder
* Open it the other way
* It's empty!

3 Close it up so that the back is showing

Open and close from left to right, just like this sequence, and you will see how it works.

4 Open it up the other way It's empty!

Remember it's front to back then back to front

5 Close it up again so that the front is showing again

Now you see how important it is for the front and back covers to look the same.

6 Finally, open it up again and the star has returned

Wands and tiaras
Magic up a fairy wand...

and wish for a glittering tiara

Magic wand

2 Take a plant stick or a length of doweling 12 in (30 cm) long. Wind a strip of colored paper or ribbon around the stick and fix it with a dab of glue at each end.

1 Cut out two star shapes from posterboard. Cover them with foil.

3 Decorate your stars with sparkly stickers and sequins.

Decorate one of your stars and and stick it to the other one, wrong sides together, with the stick fastened firmly between them.

Fairy tiara

1 Cut a paper plate in half. Draw a zigzag around the edge.

2 Carefully cut out the zigzag.

3 Place some stickers, sequins, or glitter on your tiara in the design of your choice.

4 Fix your decorations in place. Now cut a strip of posterboard that fits around your head and staple it to the tiara.

81

Paper Plate Faces

Send a chill down the spines of your neighbors when you go "trick or treating" by wearing these creepy masks made out of paper plates. Try a creepy cat, a petrified pumpkin, a wicked witch, or even a sinister skull!

Make a menacing mask from a plain paper plate

Face from a plate

Draw a face and cut it out

Add some spooky features

Attach on some elastic

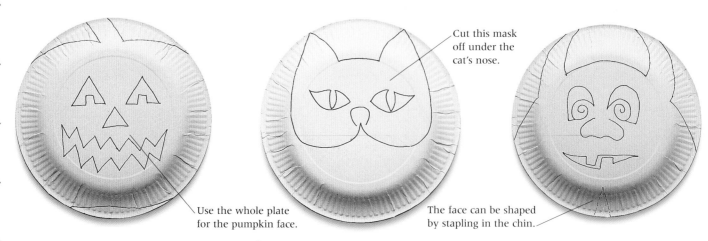

Cut this mask off under the cat's nose.

Use the whole plate for the pumpkin face.

The face can be shaped by stapling in the chin.

DECORATING PAPER PLATE FACES

Quick to make, fun to wear—these paper plate masks can be worn plain or decorated. Use any decoration you like—glitter and sequins give a great eye-catching sparkle, and different colored paints bring monsters and pumpkins to life!

Transform yourself into a paper plate monster!

Draw on your witch features.

Make some markings where you will cut and shape the face.

Cut and shape some facial features.

Snip the markings at the top and bottom, fold them in, and staple them to give you a shape.

Paint the mask, then glue on some glitter using craft glue.

ACRYLIC PAINT

CRAFT GLUE

GLITTER

Pumpkin head

Use swirly green glitter around the edge.

Black cat

Decorate the cat with glitter and sequins.

Purple monster

This monster face has green glitter spots—design your own decoration for your plate mask.

Keep away from green, warty witches!

Add green hair by cutting out a long piece of crêpe paper and cutting it into strips. Tape the finished fringe inside the mask.

☻ Wicked witch

The hair adds a lot to this warty witch. For a thicker head of hair simply add more crêpe tendrils to the back of the mask!

Fearsome Features

It's amazing how a touch of face paint can change you into a fully fanged vampire or a grinning witch's cat. Choose a suitable Halloween theme and challenge anyone to recognize you!

Shiver me timbers, give the pirate a treat!

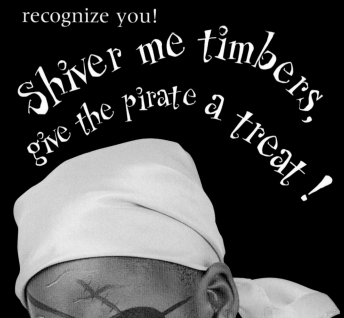

HOW TO PAINT FEARSOME FACES

Face paints are easy to use, but you have to take your time doing them to get the best result. Try experimenting with some styles on paper and then persuade a friend to let you loose on their face! Warning—face paints can be messy; you should have some towels handy!

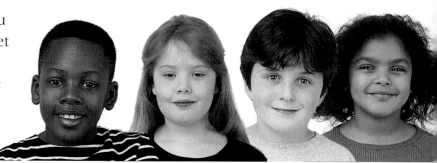

Pirate

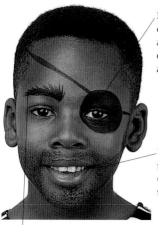

Paint a black eye patch around the eye and add a strap.

Use a coarse sponge to dab on some stubble.

Paint on a big, hairy eyebrow.

Draw some red scars and highlight them with white paint.

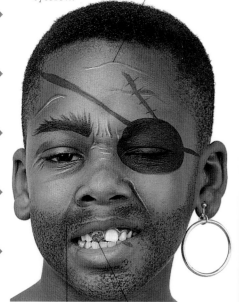

Scrunch up your face to help you to position the wrinkle lines.

Color in a black tooth with an eyeliner pencil.

Witch

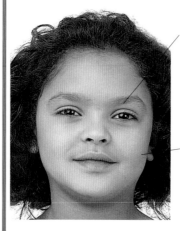

Use a pale purple for the witch-like eye-shadow.

Rub the same purple onto your cheeks as blush.

Paint on black eyebrows and use eyeliner around your eyes.

Mix black paint with the eyeshadow for the lipstick.

Add a creepy-crawly or two if you like!

Skull

Wear a black hairband to frame the face.

Sponge on a white base color.

Paint big, black eye sockets.

Blend in some yellow paint to add to the bony look.

Color the nose in black paint; note the shape.

Draw some black cracks around the face.

Create a toothy mouth with thin, black lines.

Sponge for blending colors or covering large areas.

Water-based face paint—colors can be mixed together.

Paintbrush for drawing on fine lines.

Eyeliner pencil for blacking out teeth.

Glitter for an extra highlight.

Watch out for skin allergies—test first

Black Cat

Color around the eyes using white paint.

Use a sponge to dab white paint around the mouth and chin.

Paint the nose and bottom lip pink.

Color black around the white part of the eyes.

Brush black strokes around the mouth and all over the rest of the face.

Finish the face with some strokes of silver glitter.

Scaly Monster

Start by sponging some yellow paint in the center of the face.

Dab green around the yellow and spread it over the hairline.

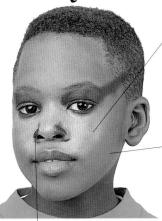

Use red for the eyeshadow and to flare the nostrils.

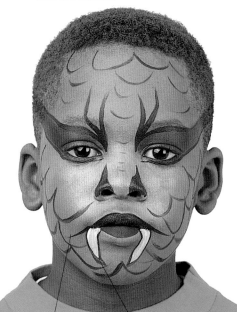

Draw on the scales, the lips, and around the eyes with black paint.

Paint on some white fang shapes and highlight them in black.

Vampire

Slick back your hair using lots of hair gel.

Dab on white paint with a sponge.

Rub some gray around the eyes for a sunken look.

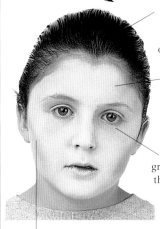

Dab some gray along the cheekbones to narrow the face.

Draw a hairline and paint it with black paint.

Paint gray around the eye sockets and add some red lines.

Color the lips and draw in some fangs dripping with red blood!

89

Hello, hands!

Forget your face, paint your hands instead! Turn your fingers into little personalities.

Face paints

Water for thinning paint.

Fine and thick brushes, and a washable felt-tip pen.

Sponges to paint large areas.

wet the sponge and dab it in the paint.

Paint your hand all over with the sponge.

Add the details with a paintbrush.

Soccer crazy

Let's go!

My ball

Yes!

I liked the sliding tackle. Good game, Jim!

Hints and tips

• Choose a good-quality face paint.
• Look at your hands and decide on a shape that suits your fingers.
• Use a damp sponge to cover large areas. Wait for it to dry before you paint the details.
• Use a washable felt-tip for outlines and faces.
• Clean the paints off with soap and water.

Pretty Polly

Creatures with beaks and long necks work well, too, like this parrot. Try other birds—a rooster or a pink flamingo.

Elephant fingers

I am an alien

New Look

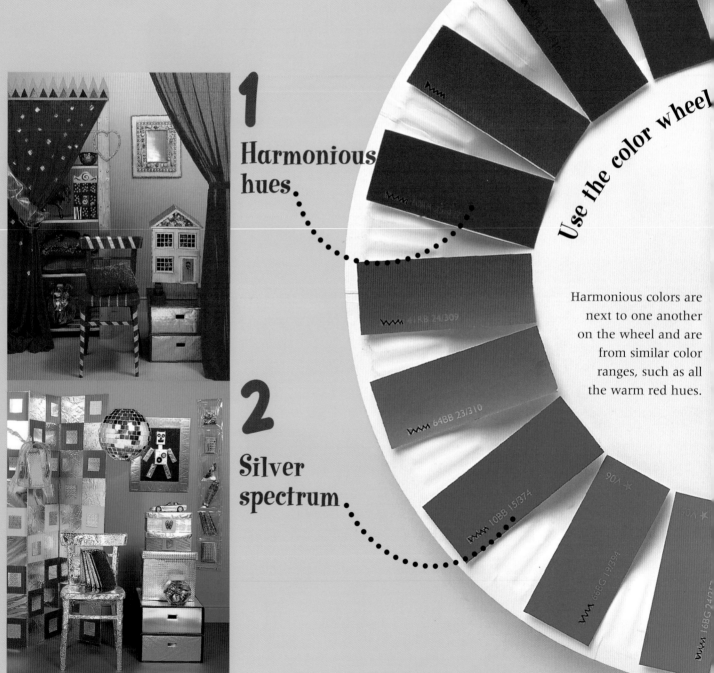

1
Harmonious hues

2
Silver spectrum

Use the color wheel

Harmonious colors are next to one another on the wheel and are from similar color ranges, such as all the warm red hues.

1RB 24/309

64BB 23/310

10BB 15/374

66BG 19/394

16BG 24/

V06

V01

Make your own color wheel by cutting swatches of paint colors up. Arrange them in order of the colors of the spectrum (red, orange, yellow, green, blue, purple) and then glue them to the rim of a paper plate.

to create your scheme.

Complementary colors are any colors from opposite sides of the wheel. They contrast with one another, such as orange and its opposites blue and green.

3
Wild contrasts

4
Sunshine shades

5
Comic colors

Changing CHAIRS

Bring a chair to life

by painting it with zebra stripes or sticking on paper butterflies and fake flowers. Give it a kick by covering it with team colors and a soccer photo. If you want to keep your chair under wraps instead of under piles of clothes, try covering it in aluminum foil, or spice it up with fake fur or a fantastic feather boa.

2

4

5

Changing Chairs

You'll need to use an old chair that no one minds you decorating. If you are not allowed to paint a chair, choose a method that just covers it up. The chair to be painted needs to be clean, so wash it with soap and water. Then collect the other things that you will need—sandpaper, a paintbrush, paint, magazine pictures, aluminum foil, fake fur, or whatever you want to use.

Wrap the sandpaper around a wooden block for extra grip.

a) If your chair is rough, rub it with sandpaper—medium-weight sandpaper works well on most wood.

Use semi-gloss latex paint for a long-lasting finish, and a brush that's about 1 1/2 in (4 cm) wide.

b) You will need to give your chair a base coat first. Paint this on roughly and then leave it to dry.

c) Your second coat is the one that shows, so keep your strokes even and don't overload your brush.

Decorating chair 1

It's fun to decorate your chair using cutouts such as flowers, butterflies, cars, or stars. You can use pictures from old magazines, posters, or your sticker collection. Cut out the shapes and then stick them on your painted chair with PVA glue. Brush them with varnish.

If any glue spills out, quickly wipe it off with a clean cloth.

Varnish the cutout pictures to protect them and make them sparkle.

Decorating chair 2

Paint the chair in one of your team's colors. Then cut out strips of paper in the team's other colors. Make sure you have the right lengths to wrap around the chair. Brush the strips with PVA glue and stick them carefully onto the chair, one color at a time. Smooth them in place.

A bold pictu[re] makes a g[ood] focal poi[nt]

Your paper strips should be about 1 1/2 in (4 cm) wide.

Make the joints at the back of the chair or underneath it where they won't show.

Decorating chair 3

Animals have amazing markings and you can copy or adapt them. Use a picture for reference—choose one that clearly shows the animal's pattern. Paint your chair in one of the animal's basic colors. Draw on the markings in pencil and fill them in with acrylic paint.

Animals with strong, clear markings are easiest to copy.

Make sure the base coat is dry before you draw on your design.

Use a fine paintbrush to keep the design neat.

Decorating chair 4

Concoct an instant transformation by covering your chair with aluminum foil. Tear off pieces of foil and scrunch them into position. Secure any stray ends with clear tape. Instead of aluminum foil, you can use this method with fabric, brown wrapping paper, or colorful gift wrap.

Use clear tape to hold the aluminum foil in place.

Scrunch the foil tightly round the chair to completely cover it.

Decorating chair 5

Give your chair a new look and feel by adding an interesting texture. Feathery fake fur looks exotic, especially when it's an electric color. Simply tape down one end, wrap the fur around the chair and secure.

Long pieces of fake fur are easier to work with than short pieces.

Experiment with designs before you stick the fur into place.

Decorating DOORKNOBS

Make your mark on the door to your room by decorating your doorknob. You can hint at a theme inside your room—seascapes, polka dots, or glitzy glamour —or discourage visitors from bugging you. Mix and match colors and textures so your doorknobs look and feel great! Then try out your ideas on closet and chest-of-drawer handles, too.

Use ready-mixed, all-purpose spackle.

a) Spread spackle straight onto the knob. Spread newspaper underneath to catch any blobs.

b) Gently press decorations into the spackle. Leave the knob to dry for about 30 minutes.

Acrylic paint is the best type to use.

c) When the spackle is dry, use a fine artist's brush to cover it with gold paint.

For the seashore look, press shells into the spackle. To finish, brush on a water-based varnish.

Paint your knobs with a bright acrylic paint, and then glue on anything you like!

Stick bits of colored foil and candy wrappers onto the knob for a bright, theatrical effect.

Get down to the nuts and bolts by sticking them on with craft glue and painting with varnish.

Choose a small handful of multicolored beads for a perfect Aladdin appearance.

A is for "anything goes" when it comes to giving a personal touch to your room.

Buttons give instant color. Glue them onto a plain knob, and coat with varnish.

Dot your doorknob with simple stickers. Brush with varnish to keep the spots in place.

Keep out! Varnished bugs, beasts, or aliens give unwanted guests the creeps.

Bright
IDEAS

Throw some new light

on your room by transforming any plain lamp shade. You can stick on anything from spots to snakes, paint it with stripes or swirls, cover it with cutouts, or sew on glimmering jewels. It will look fun, and the atmosphere of the whole room will change for the better.

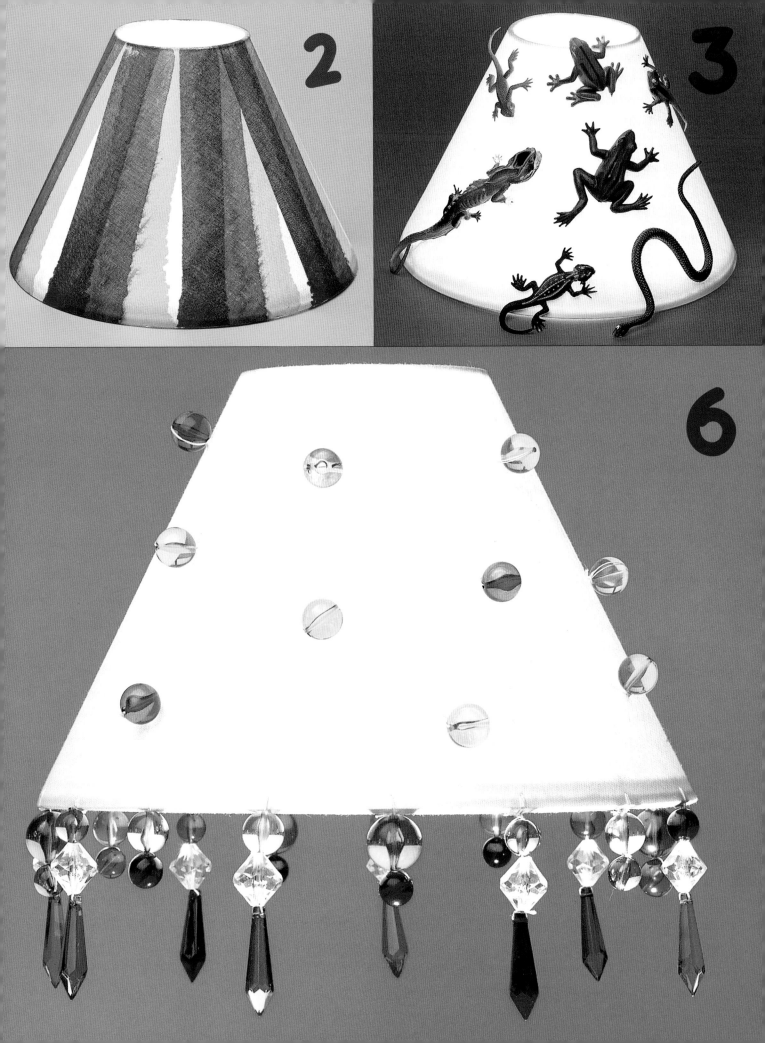

Bright Ideas

First, unplug the lamp and detach the shade before you start. If it's a hanging shade, you may need help getting it down. Whatever design you choose, always leave the top uncovered to allow the bulb's heat to escape. Depending on the look you want, you will need to find some cardboard, silk dyes, fabric paints, felt-tip pens, glue, a paintbrush, or some beads.

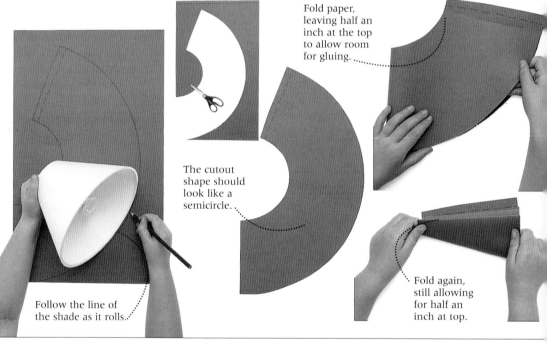

Glue the shapes on with a glue stick.

Decorating lamp 1

For animal prints, like this cheetah pattern, look for a photograph you can copy, and then draw the shapes onto black cardboard. Cut these out and glue them onto a plain white or cream-colored shade.

Decorating lamp 5

You can make your own paper shade to slip over an existing one so that the light shines though a pattern of cutouts. Roll the shade over a sheet of paper, drawing its outline. Cut out the shade shape and fold it in half. Fold it again. Leave a space at the top for gluing, and cut shapes out of the two folded edges. Glue the outer edges together and slip the cover over your original shade.

Follow the line of the shade as it rolls.

Fold paper, leaving half an inch at the top to allow room for gluing.

The cutout shape should look like a semicircle.

Fold again, still allowing for half an inch at top.

Decorating lamp 6

For this lamp, sew single glass beads directly onto the fabric of your shade. To attach the beads around the rim, thread several together as shown and then pass the needle through the beads again before sewing them onto the rim of the shade. Try alternating long beads and round ones for the edge.

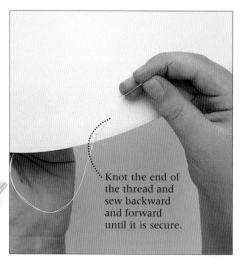

Knot the end of the thread and sew backward and forward until it is secure.

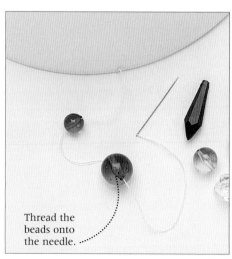

Thread the beads onto the needle.

Decorating lamp 2

Painting the shade with silk dyes or fabric paints is one of the easiest ways to transform your lamp. You can practice a design on some old fabric beforehand. If you don't have dyes or paint, try using thick felt-tip pens.

Paint the colors so they blend together.

Decorating lamp 3

For a dramatic or creepy effect, glue bugs, beasts, or bats to your lamp shade. Toy shops usually sell cheap collections of plastic animals that you can stick on with craft glue.

Spread the glue along the whole length of the animal to hold it securely in place.

Decorating lamp 4

For an illuminated stained-glass effect, glue colored tissue paper or cellophane to the back of the shade, covering the cutouts.

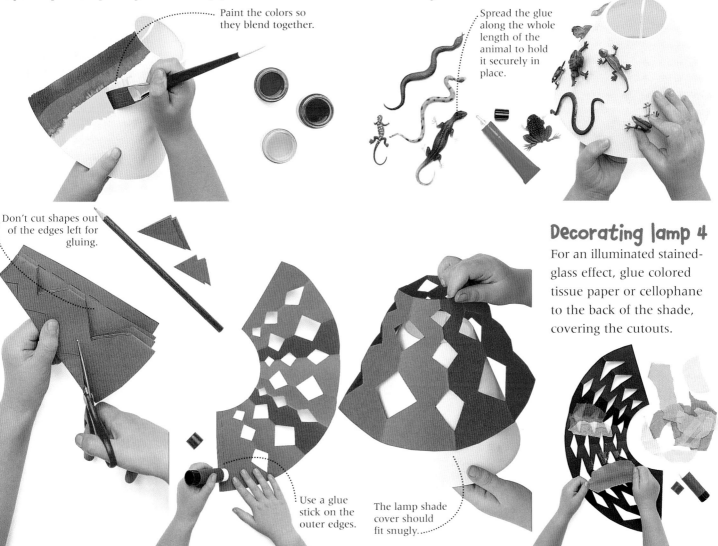

Don't cut shapes out of the edges left for gluing.

Use a glue stick on the outer edges.

The lamp shade cover should fit snugly.

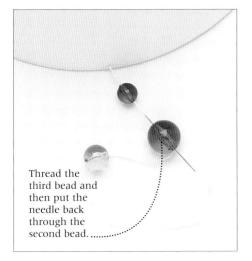

Thread the third bead and then put the needle back through the second bead.

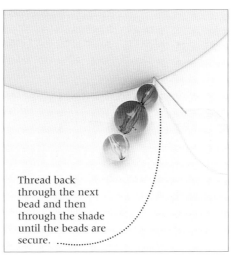

Thread back through the next bead and then through the shade until the beads are secure.

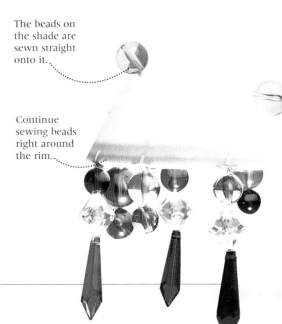

The beads on the shade are sewn straight onto it.

Continue sewing beads right around the rim.

Big SCREENS

Beads, bugs, buttons,

as well as hundreds of colorful straws—these are some of the ingredients you can use for a brilliant range of blinds or screens. Hang them over your window, a bookcase, or set of shelves.

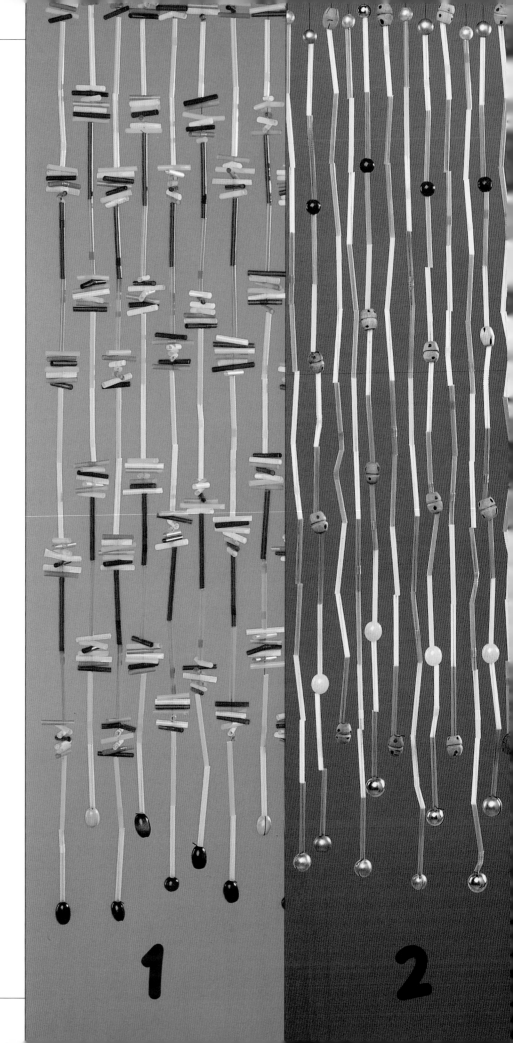

1

2

3

4

Making Screens

First you will need to measure the height and width of the area to be covered by your screen. It's a good idea to measure twice to make sure you get the right measurement. Then allow about 1 in (3 cm) extra all around. Choose a dowel or bamboo pole that is wider than the screen you want to make. Paint it with an acrylic paint that complements the colors you choose for the screen. Leave the pole until it is completely dry.

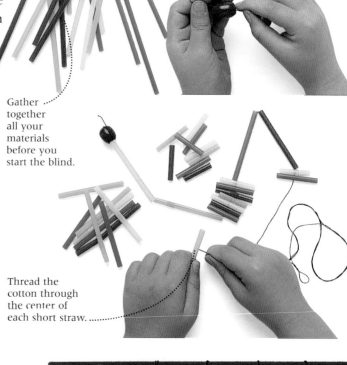

Gather together all your materials before you start the blind.

You'll need to screw hooks into a window frame to hold the blind.

Making screen 1

Measure out a long piece of strong thread. Thread the needle; then pass it through a wooden bead. Tie the bead in place with a secure knot. Cut the straws into different lengths, and pass the needle through two longer ones. Make a bundle of six or seven short lengths, lay them horizontally, and pierce them with the needle. Continue the pattern, leaving enough thread to attach the line to the pole. When finished, hang the screen on the hooks.

Thread the cotton through the center of each short straw.

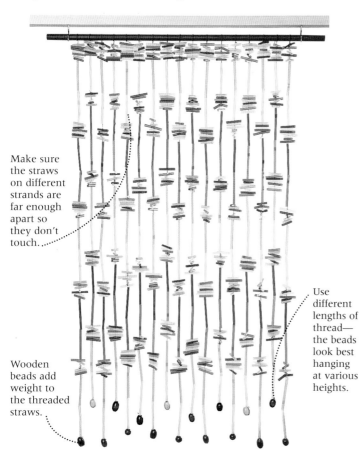

Make sure the straws on different strands are far enough apart so they don't touch.

Wooden beads add weight to the threaded straws.

Use different lengths of thread—the beads look best hanging at various heights.

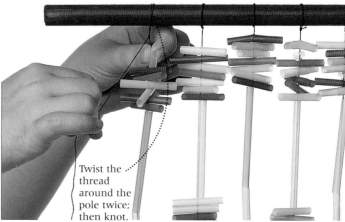

Twist the thread around the pole twice; then knot.

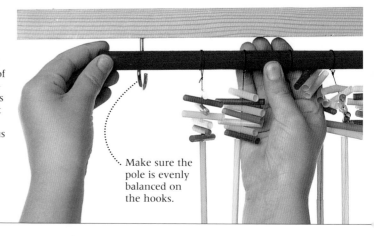

Make sure the pole is evenly balanced on the hooks.

Making screen 2

Secure a bead on the end of your thread. Then alternate colored straws and add another bead. Continue in this way until the thread is covered. Other strands can have colored straws and just a couple of beads.

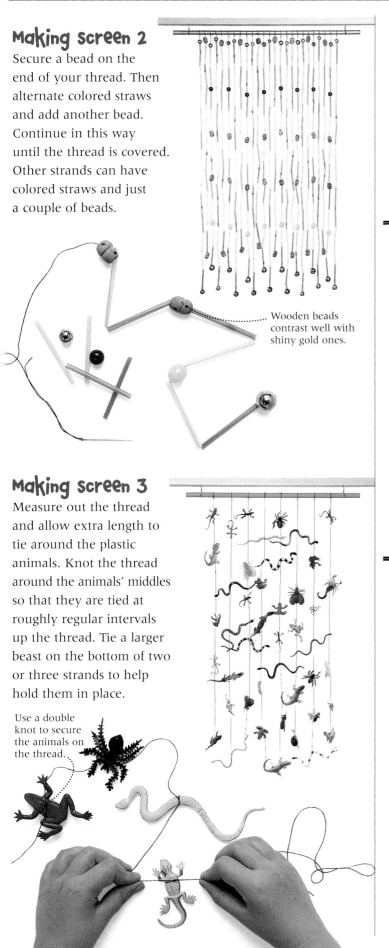

Wooden beads contrast well with shiny gold ones.

Making screen 3

Measure out the thread and allow extra length to tie around the plastic animals. Knot the thread around the animals' middles so that they are tied at roughly regular intervals up the thread. Tie a larger beast on the bottom of two or three strands to help hold them in place.

Use a double knot to secure the animals on the thread.

Making screen 4

Cut out a piece of transparent material such as muslin, bubble wrap, or bold-colored tulle. Allow about 1 1/2 in (4 cm) of extra length at the top to wrap around the pole. Lay your material out flat and smooth out any wrinkles; then attach it to the pole using blobs of PVA glue. Use colorful candy wrappers, buttons, and bits of foil to decorate the rest of the screen.

Make your basic blind before you begin to decorate.

Attach foil shapes to hide any blobs of glue.

Lay out your design before you stick it all in place.

The candy wrapper edges give the blind colorful symmetry.

When it hangs against the light the material appears see-through.

PICTURE Frames

Put yourself in the picture by making incredible frames for your favorite photos. Make a collage, or use fake fur and silky sunflowers to brighten up your room. Pick colorful beads to create a jeweled effect. Try framing a mirror.

1

2

3

4

5

Picture Frames
Making the basic frame

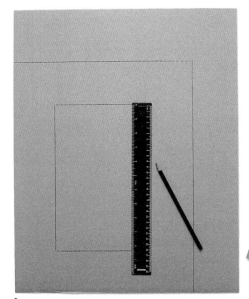

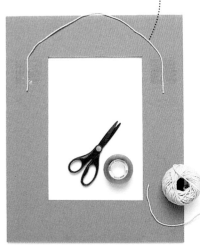

The frame will hang best if you stick the string to the top part of it.

a) Measure out a frame on a large sheet of cardboard. Make it wide enough—about 3 in (8 cm)—to create a design.

b) Cut out the frame using a ruler and craft knife. Keep the middle window smaller than the picture to be framed.

c) Tape string to the back, or if the frame is heavy, knot string through holes in the cardboard.

You can use any object that will stick.

Things that are the same shape make a good border.

Making frame 1

Collect together small objects such as pasta bows and old toys. Lay them out on the frame—a roughly symmetrical pattern works best. Once you are happy with the result, stick the pieces down with craft glue. Lay the frame on newspaper, and spray with gold paint.

Making frame 2

Spread craft glue on the cardboard. Stick the cardboard to the fake fur. Trim the corners of the fur. Cut an X in the fabric inside the frame; then trim the fabric and glue it in place. Attach string and decorate.

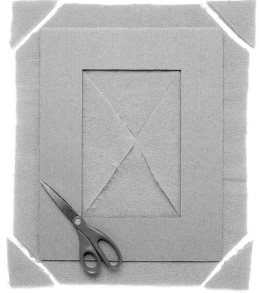

The glue shouldn't be too thick.

Choose light fabric flowers to stick to the front of your frame.

Making frames 3 and 4

Cut out your basic frame; then choose colorful magazine pages and tear or cut them into strips. Cut out pictures of sports heroes, cartoon characters, or other images. Lay the strips over the frame and glue them in position, wrapping the ends around the back. Stick the cutout characters over these to create an action-packed collage. You could try the same thing with pictures of stars from favorite movies and bands.

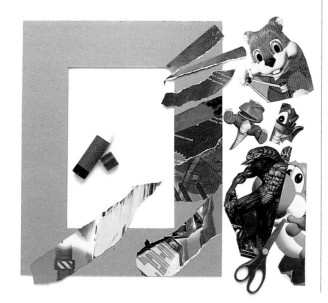

Making frame 5

Cut out small squares of cardboard that are as wide as your frame. Use craft glue to stick them neatly around the frame. Next paint the frame with gold acrylic paint. When the paint is dry, glue on shiny beads and bright buttons.

Adding layers of cardboard will make a simple frame more interesting.

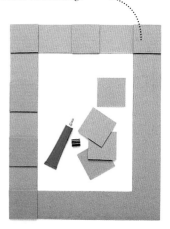

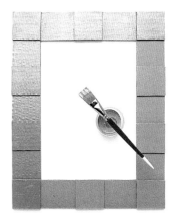

Paint or Dye

Transform white cotton

fabric by using paint or dye. Make rainbow stripes, spiral shapes, or bright checks. And for circles and swirls, knot up your material for tie-dye. Once you create your unique designs, sew different pieces together to make anything from pillow covers to bedspreads.

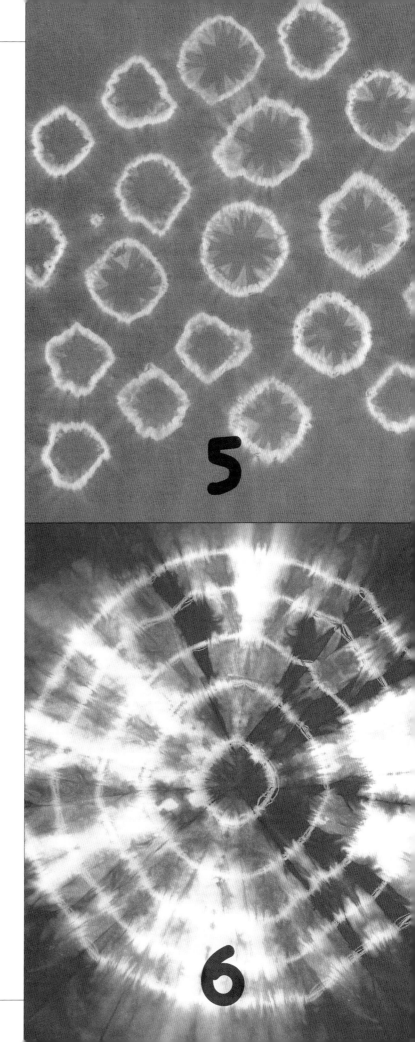

5

6

Paint or Dye
Painting fabric

Start off by choosing a piece of fabric—100% cotton is best because it is cheap and it takes dye well. Paint on your designs using silk dyes. These are very runny and blend together for some unexpected results. Painting fabric can be messy, so protect your work surface by covering it with several layers of newspaper. Cut your fabric into a manageable size; then lay it flat on the newspaper. Use tape to secure it in place. Choose a medium-size paintbrush and make sure it is perfectly clean before you dip it in the silk dye.

Paint or dye 2, 3, and 4

Paint the stripes from top to bottom for a clear view of your work.

Paint or dye 1

Paint a spiral pattern from the middle outward, one color at a time. Let the colors run together for a well-blended look.

a) Load up your brush; then paint colored lines onto the fabric. Try to space the lines at regular intervals.

Dyeing fabric

This tie-dyeing pattern is made using a cold-water dye. The steps shown here are a general guide, but make sure you follow the method described on the dye package. Use cotton fabric since this absorbs the dye best. And always wear rubber gloves when you handle the wet cotton, since the dye will stain your skin.

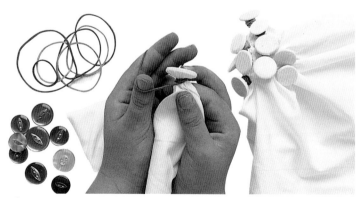

Paint or dye 5 and 6

Any area of the fabric bound by rubber bands or string will not absorb the dye and will remain white. One method of tie-dyeing is to tie buttons into the fabric. This leaves you with a pattern of small circles.

a) Puncture the container of dye and sprinkle the powder into a quart of water. Let the dye dissolve.

b) Add the bag of fixative and the required quantity of salt. Stir the mixture until everything is dissolved.

Choose bright, strong colors for a dramatic effect.

b) Before each set of lines is dry, begin the next color. It doesn't matter if your lines are not perfectly straight.

Leave some fabric unpainted for bright, white markings.

Make sure you don't rest your wrist on the wet paint.

c) Paint vertical stripes or dots in the spaces. Or try painting more horizontal stripes. Iron the fabric to set the dyes.

c) Pour the dye mixture into a bowl of warm water. Stir contents of bowl until thoroughly mixed.

d) Immerse your tied-up fabric in the dye. Make sure it is completely soaked. Then leave it for one hour.

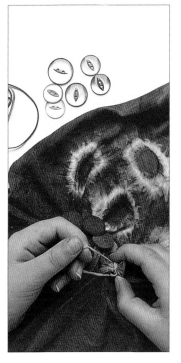

e) Squeeze out the fabric and rinse away the excess dye. Let the fabric dry and then remove the buttons.

You can make different tie-dye designs by changing the way you tie the rubber bands. For a hoop design, fold fabric from the middle and tie rubber bands at intervals.

Personalize PILLOWS

whether you go for junk-filled bubble wrap or brilliant bows, colorful cacti or sparkling tinsel, rainbow stripes or zebra patterns, you can reinvent the pillows for your bedroom. Bright colors and cool designs will work wonders—they'll add life to an old chair, a dull corner, or a tired bed.

1

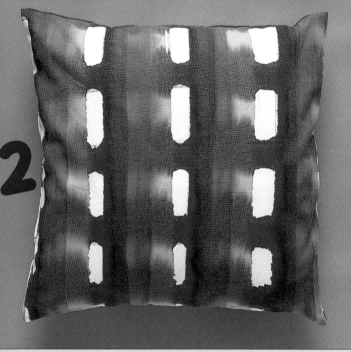

2

3

4

5

6

Personalize Pillows
Making a pillow cover

You can customize a ready-made pillow cover, but if you want to make one of your own, here's how. Start by cutting out two pieces of fabric that are about 14 x 14 in (35 x 35 cm), or the size that will fit an existing pillow. Pin these together. Starting about half an inch (1.5 cm) from the edge, sew the two pieces together. Leave a 10-in (25-cm) space on one edge to allow room for the pillow. Trim off the corners, then turn the case inside out. Push in pillow stuffing and neatly sew up the open edge.

Pin the fabric together with the right sides facing each other.

Pillow 1

Pillow covers don't need to be made from fabric, so why not experiment? Bubble wrap, for example, makes an unusual pillow. Cut out a long, oblong piece—12 x 24 in (30 x 60 cm) is about the right size for a small pillow. Tape two of the open sides together, and then fill the pillow with empty potato chip bags, candy wrappers, fabric, or any other soft, colorful item you have around. Once the pillow is full, tape it up.

The piece of bubble wrap should be twice the width of the pillow you want to make.

Bring the sides to meet in the middle.

Use clear tape to stick the edges together.

Don't overfill the bag or the seams will split.

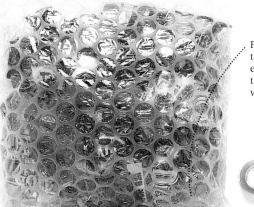

Fold over the open edges, and then seal with tape.

Use small, neat stitches to sew up the cushion. ....

Be careful not to trim the corners close to the stitches or you will make a hole.

Push the corners into points when you turn the case right side out. ....

Make sure you don't tear the cover when you stuff it.

Use matching thread to sew the gap closed. ....

Use material with interesting textures. ....

Wrap the ribbon around the pillow like you would around a present. .....

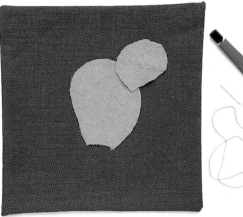

Pillows 2 and 4

Use the fabric you designed using paint or dye to make colorful pillow covers. For an even brighter variation, add a ribbon, tied in a simple bow.

Pillow 3

Cut out shapes from scrap material and glue them onto the fabric. Use bold stitches to help hold the fabric in place—they can become part of the design, too.

Curl the tinsel into balls before sewing it on the pillow.

Stick the stripes on with craft glue.

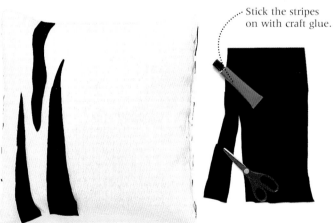

Pillow 5

Sew a piece of tinsel around the edge of the pillow, and then sew more tinsel onto the front and back. Try using ribbons, buttons, or pieces of fake fur.

Pillow 6

Create a dramatic animal pattern, such as these zebra stripes. Simply cut out strips from a piece of felt and glue them straight onto the pillow cover.

Cover up!

Wear your art on your clothes,
and keep the sun off, too!

GraffiT-shirt
Make your mark

Fabric pens are the easiest way to decorate a T-shirt. Draw your design right on, then iron it to make it permanent.

Remember to put paper or cardboard inside the T-shirt to stop the ink from going through.

You will need:
- White or light-colored cotton T-shirt
- Fabric pens

I'm looking at you!

T-shirts

White and pale-colored T-shirts work best when decorating or dying. If you use a dark T-shirt, the decoration won't show as clearly. So get out your old T-shirts and cover up!

Hey! look at me I look good like that

Pack up all your stuff in me!

Transform your clothes

Crazy faces

You could use any material to decorate your hats and bags, but felt is a great fabric to use—it is easy to cut and can be stuck onto other material with white glue or fabric glue.

Practice your face shapes on newspaper first. Then cut them out.

Use the paper templates to draw on the fabric.

Cut out the shapes.

what to do
• Practice your shapes on a piece of newspaper.
• Use your newspaper template to cut out the felt shapes.
• Glue them into position.

Glue the shapes.

white glue

Stick in position.

You will need:
• Scraps of fabric, such as felt
• Newspaper
• Scissors
• PVA or white glue

122

Tie-dye T-shirts

The secret to tie-dye is the elastic bands. If they are tied tightly, the dye will not color the tied parts, leaving swirls of pattern. When you are dying fabrics, make sure you read and follow the instructions on the dye package.

⭐ **Ask an adult** to help with hot water.

Tie the bands

Scrunch up pieces of your T-shirt and tie elastic bands tightly to each little scrunch.

Follow the guidelines on the package.

Now dunk your T-shirt into the dye and leave for however long the instructions tell you. Use rubber gloves.

Take it out and rinse it

Mix up the dye

Dunk in a T-shirt

Remove the bands

Rinse the T-shirt until the colour stops running out. Remove the elastic bands to reveal the twisty, swirly pattern. Then hang it up in the sun to dry.

Remember to use a light T-shirt; otherwise, the dye won't show.

The more elastic bands you use, the more patterns you get.

HANDy Hangers

Add character to your closet

by creating some humorous hangers. Your clothes will never look the same once they are draped over the shoulders of mixed-up models, anxious aliens, or mad, masked animals. Make the base, and then do your own thing.

Use cutouts fro magazines to sti over one anoth and create abstract fac

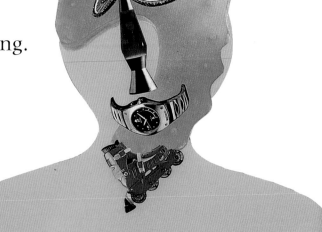

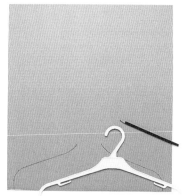

a) Lay a hanger on stiff cardboard and trace around it to make the shoulders and neck.

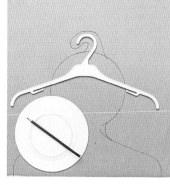

b) Trace a small plate for the head, adding a thickened hook from the top of the hanger.

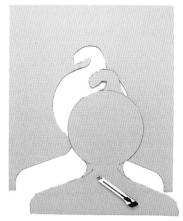

c) Cut out the whole shape with a craft knife. Remember to cut on a rubber mat.

d) Use cutouts of facial features from magazines to create a crazy fashion victim.

Mix together pictures of stars with computer images for a weird collage portrait.

Stick a different shape over the face of the hanger; paint it green; and give it huge eyes for an alien encounter.

Each distorted glamour girl will be different when you create a collage of caricatured features.

Once you've painted on fur patterns, attach masks to make dramatic heads for animal hangers—they're a little spooky, too.

For simple silliness, just paint your hanger and glue on a pair of joke glasses.

Decorations

Hang'em high

Party banners

These decorations are simple and quick to put together using two or three basic shapes that suit your theme.

All you need are string, straws, and your paper shapes

Cut a piece of string the length you want your banner to be, and tie a knot at one end.

Thread the string through the straw...

...then through the first paper shape.

Flags and streamers

Create a party atmosphere by hanging fluttering flags and swishing streamers around your house or yard.

Have a race using the streamers

Bags of flags

All you need for the best bunting is lots and lots of colorful plastic bags.

1 Find your most colorful plastic bags.

2 Cut out lots and lots of triangle shapes.

3 Fold each one over a piece of string and staple in place.

Fluttering streamers

Cut plastic bags into strips to make streamers that flutter in the wind! Hang them outside your front door to show where the party is.

Ask an Adult to help

Tape each one to a plastic strip 2 in (5 cm) wide.

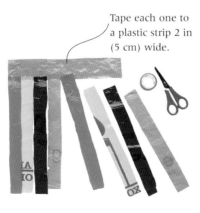

1 Cut a plastic bottle into 2-in (5-cm) bands.

2 Cut lots of plastic bags into long strips

3 Wrap one strip around the plastic band.

4 Attach some string to the end and hang it up.

Paper Chains

Screaming streamers are easy to make and a perfect decoration to hang around a table or on a wall on Hallowe'en. Careful when you cut them, you don't want to separate your pumpkins or "nose to nose" cats!

Cut out a long strip of paper, 8 in. (10 cm) wide and however long you want, and fold it backward and forward in a square shape to make an accordion effect.

Folded edge —

Folded edge

Folded edge —

Draw your ghost design on the surface, making sure it runs to each folded edge.

Cut the ghost out leaving a part of the folded edges of each side uncut so that the ghosts are holding hands when you pull the paper apart.

Pull it out, decorate it, and hang it up!

Flickering Flashlights

As dusk falls on Allhallows' eve it's time to create some shadowy light to guide the ghosts, spirits, and even yourself around your area. Jazz up your flashlight and decorate a jar to hang on a branch.

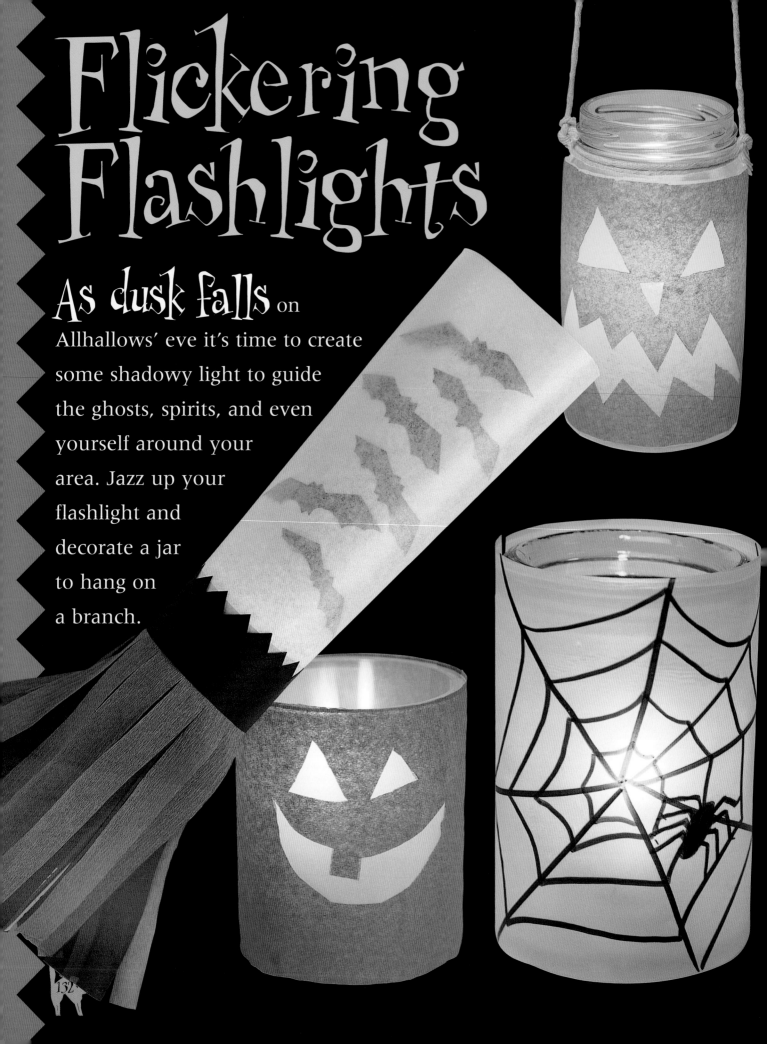

Wend Your Way at **witching hour** in creepy **candlelight**

How to Make Jeering Jars

Collect some glass jars or vases, any shape or size, and some bright tissue or plain tracing paper, and you are ready to start making your jeering jars and flickering flashlights! Small candles with flat bottoms are the safest candles to use and give a good flicker when placed inside your creepy jars. When you light them, make sure you ask someone to help you.

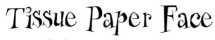
★ **Ask an adult ...**
to light the candle

Tissue Paper Face

A simple face is a great pattern to use. The candle shimmering through the features will drive off any wandering spirits!

Cut some tissue paper to fit the jar.

Draw a face and cut it out.

Ask an adult to tie string securely around the rim, light a candle inside, and hang it up!

Tape the tissue to the jar.

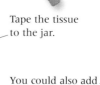

You could also add a layer of yellow tissue under the cutout face.

134

Night Jar

Another way to decorate a jar is to use tracing paper. Either use a marker to draw a picture on the paper, or cut out shapes from black card and stick them on. Wrap the paper around the jar and light the candle!

Cut out black shapes and stick them to the paper.

Draw a picture on the paper using a black marker.

Flashy Flashlight

Your friends will be green with envy when you flash your new light! Take it outside at dusk to see its full effect!

Cut tracing paper to fit around the flashlight with a 8-in. lengthwise.

Cut spooky shapes out of black paper and stick them on.

Wrap the paper around the end of the light with the shapes on the inside.

Tape down the seam.

Cut a frill out of crêpe paper and stick it around the handle.

Turn it on and you're ready to go!

monster mobiles

Hang your own reptiles

Create cardboard cutouts of your favorite dinosaurs. Now add faces and details, string them up, and watch them turn in the breeze.

Twirly t-rex

This scary meat-eater has claws, big teeth, and a spiny back.

Thread some string through each body section and attach them to the string with a piece of tape.

real diplos were nearly 90 ft (30 m) long!

Dangly diplodocus

Diplodocus was a huge, two-legged dinosaur with a very small brain!

trailing pterosaur

These leathery meat-eaters looked a bit like bats—try hanging a few around your "cave."

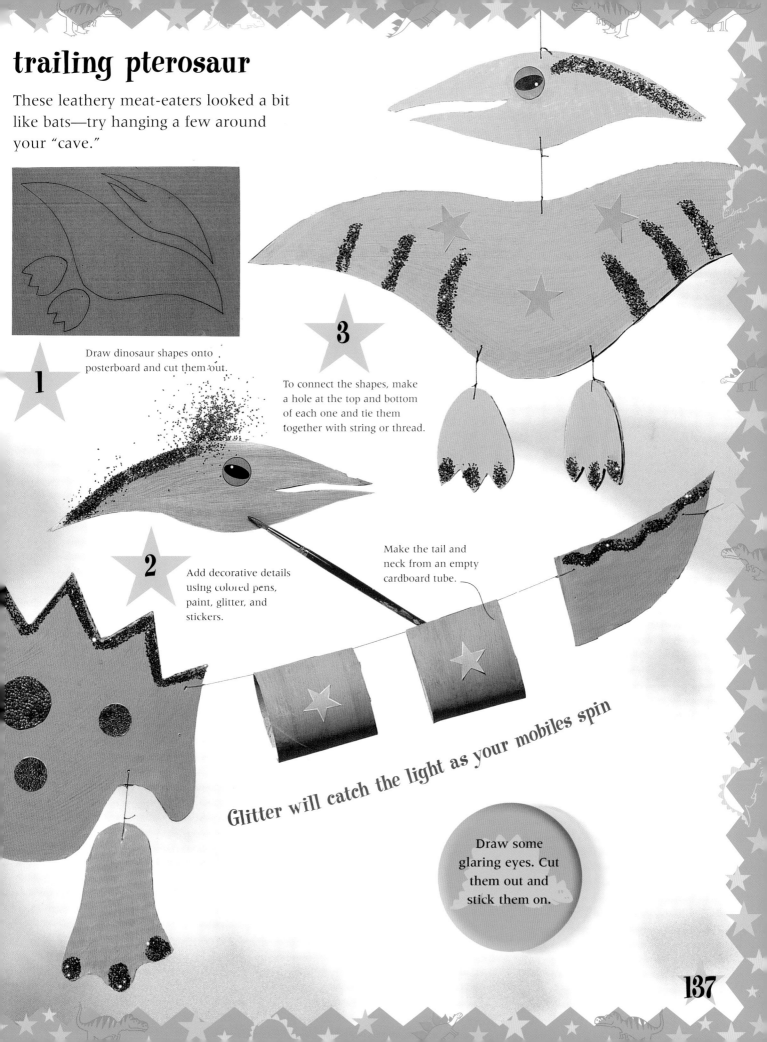

1 Draw dinosaur shapes onto posterboard and cut them out.

2 Add decorative details using colored pens, paint, glitter, and stickers.

3 To connect the shapes, make a hole at the top and bottom of each one and tie them together with string or thread.

Make the tail and neck from an empty cardboard tube.

Glitter will catch the light as your mobiles spin

Draw some glaring eyes. Cut them out and stick them on.

Merry Mobiles

Christmas is on the move.

Hang Rudolphs, Santas, wintry snowmen, and tree faces around your room and you'll be spinning!

Cut out shapes from cardboard and jazz them up

Use cardboard for your mobiles.

Glitter will catch the light when the mobiles spin and give the room an extra sparkle.

Paint the eyes

These ornaments make great tree eyes.

Give the nose an extra sparkle

Table-tennis ball eyes.

Make a hole at the top and bottom, thread some string through, and knot.

Feeling dizzy yet?

It's meltdown for the snowman!

✰ In a Spin

Hang these fantastic mobiles from the ceiling and watch them spinning and twirling around. Remember to paint and decorate them on both sides so that whichever way they turn you can see exactly what they are.

139

Festive windows

Day and night, give your room a Christmassy glow with these tissue paper windows

1

SCISSORS

PENCIL

Draw your picture on a sheet of dark-colored posterboard, and cut out some shapes.

2

Glue pieces of tissue to the back of the picture.

GLUE STICK

COLORED TISSUE PAPER

3
Turn your picture back over.

Now stick your silhouette in the window and let it shine out!

Clever cutouts

Instead of a picture, try cutting out a snowflake from folded paper. Turn to page 144 to find out how to make one.

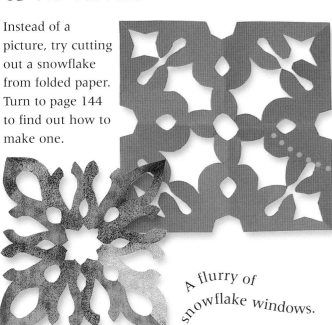

A flurry of snowflake windows.

141

Fairy angels

Twinkle, twinkle little angels
Hanging on the Christmas tree.
Paper fairies bright with glitter
Wave their starry wands at me.

1

Cut out your shape

You'll need one paper plate for each angel. On the front, draw a pencil outline that looks like this, and cut along the lines.

2

Put your decorations on the other side of the plate.

Glitter

Sequins

Add sparkly details

3

You only need one staple here.

Staple the skirt

Fairies look pretty in pink hearts and flowers.

Paper Snow

A flurry of paper snowflakes

float and swirl through the sky, settling in the branches of the trees.

Take a piece of paper and fold it in half twice along the dotted lines.

Your paper will look like this.

Fold it in half again.

Snowstorms of snowflakes!

Hang up your snowflake with thread.

Now snip away, then unfold the flake.

See what shapes unfold

Baubles,

... stars, and 3D trees

Make them small to hang on a tree

or huge to hang from the ceiling,

but whatever you do, hang them up!

3D trees

For a 3D look, slot two shapes together. Try two circles as well to give a bauble effect.

1. Cut two tree shapes exactly the same.

Cut a slot in one tree from the top to halfway down.

2. Now cut a slot in the other tree.

Cut up from base to halfway up

3. Slide one shape onto the other.

4. Stand your tree up, or stick on some thread and hang on the tree.

Paper baubles

If you use old, recycled Christmas cards, all the decorations will be completely different. You could also use your homemade printed paper.

Little or large

String me up and hang me up

How to make baubles and stars

For baubles you will need

Old greeting cards • Thick paper • Ruler • Pen • Scissors •
Hole punch • Paper fasteners • Thread

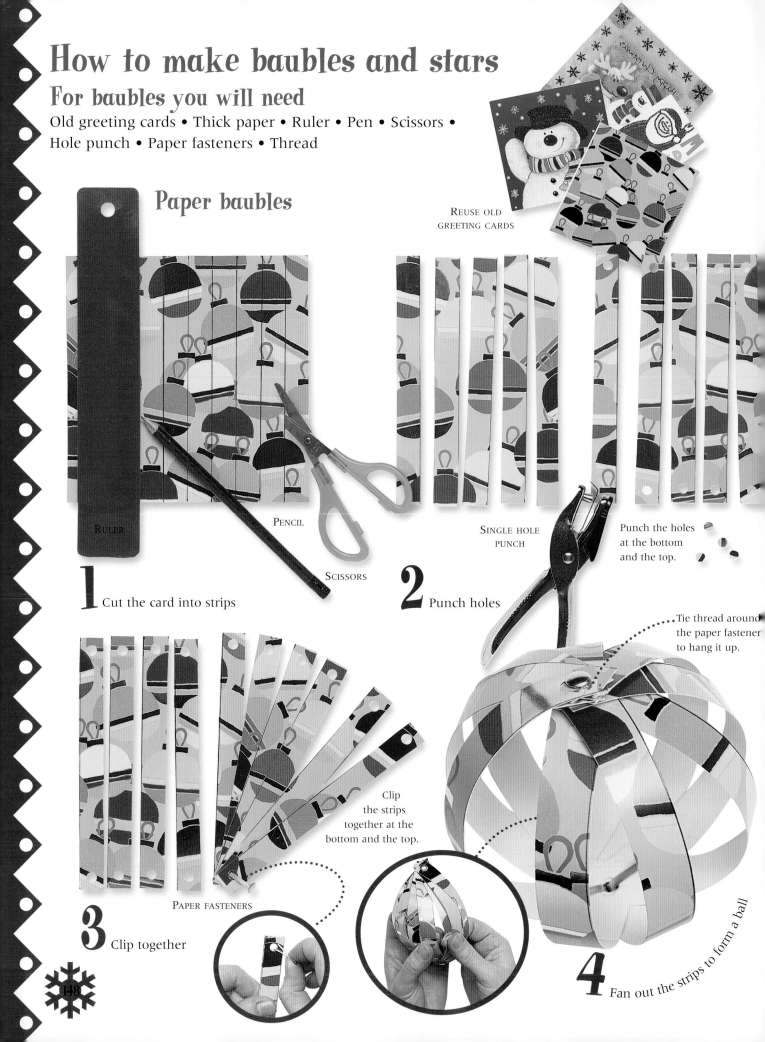

REUSE OLD
GREETING CARDS

Paper baubles

RULER

PENCIL

SCISSORS

1 Cut the card into strips

SINGLE HOLE
PUNCH

Punch the holes
at the bottom
and the top.

2 Punch holes

Tie thread around
the paper fastener
to hang it up.

PAPER FASTENERS

Clip
the strips
together at the
bottom and the top.

3 Clip together

4 Fan out the strips to form a ball

Super stars

You will need:
Paper • Pen • Scissors • Thread • Tape

Use a piece of paper measuring 8½ in (22 cm) x 11 in (28 cm).

1 Take a piece of paper

Fold the paper backward and forward like an accordion. Make the folds about 1 in (2 cm) wide.

Fold the folded paper in half.

2 Fold into pleats

Unfold the paper and draw lines to show where cut out the holes.

3 Cut some holes

Fan out the paper and tape the sides together.

4 Tape the edge

Tape the other side to complete the circle, then add a piece of string to hang it up.

5 It's a star

HOW TO MAKE POM-PONS AND BAUBLES

Paper Pom-pons

Pom-pons can be made out of any paper you like. Christmas wrapping paper is jolly and bright, or you could decorate your own paper with a Christmas pattern using paint or stickers.

Cut out eight discs of paper (about template size below).

Fold the bunch of discs in half and staple down the crease.

Baubles and Orbs

Festive baubles can be hung on trees or simply left to spin from ceilings. When you have mastered the bauble, try making the spectacular, giant orb with 20 decorated paper plates. You'll have your work cut out finding room for something that big!

Take a stack of old Christmas cards and trace around the template.

Cut out 20 circles, and snip out the notches—see template.

Use this template to cut out 20 discs

notch

FOLD HERE

FOLD HERE

Trace this triangle over the template and draw it onto each piece of construction paper.

notch

FOLD HERE

notch

150

To help you fold, run a blunt-ended pen down the dotted lines.

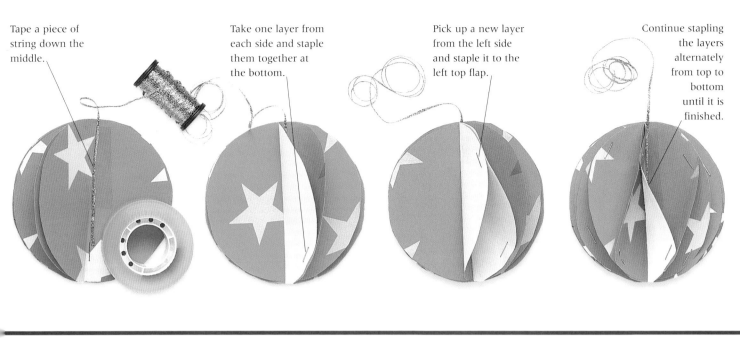

Tape a piece of string down the middle.

Take one layer from each side and staple them together at the bottom.

Pick up a new layer from the left side and staple it to the left top flap.

Continue stapling the layers alternately from top to bottom until it is finished.

Staple the flaps together at each end. Keep stapling them together until they become an orb shape.

To hang up your bauble, make a hole and tie some string through it.

Make a giant orb using 20 paper plates.

Wow! it's almost as big as me!

Winter woollies

Soft and squashy felt decorations hang around with fuzzy pom-pons.

How to stitch some woollies

Collect some colorful felts and threads. Cut out two shapes, sew them up using blanket stitch, stuff them with something soft, and decorate with sparkly sequins. Turn to page 38 to make pom-pons.

NEEDLE-THREADER

GOLD OR SILVER THREAD

LOTS OF DIFFERENT COLORED FELT

SEQUINS AND RIBBONS FOR DECORATION

Needles and pins

You will need:
• embroidery needles (use a needle-threader to help you thread a needle)
• Glue
• Stuffing

PINS

COLORED EMBROIDERY FLOSS OR THIN YARN

WHITE GLUE

SCISSORS

POLYFILL

Cutting shapes

Make some shape templates.

Draw a circle, a heart, and a triangle shape onto paper. Make the triangle shape slightly taller. Then cut them out and use them as your templates.........

Glue a heart to the triangle shape.

Angels and fairies

Cut out, stitch, and stuff

Pin your template onto a piece of folded felt and cut it out.

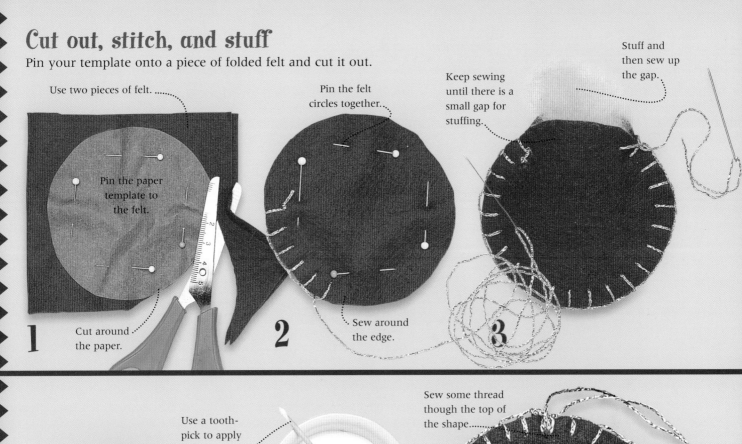

Use two pieces of felt.

Pin the paper template to the felt.

1 Cut around the paper.

Pin the felt circles together.

2 Sew around the edge.

Keep sewing until there is a small gap for stuffing.

Stuff and then sew up the gap.

3

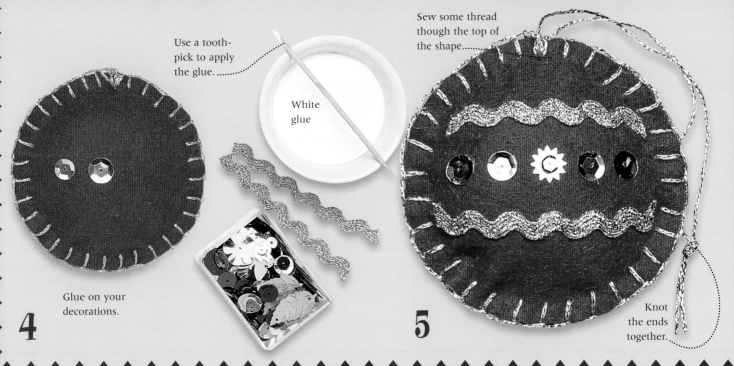

Use a tooth-pick to apply the glue.

White glue

4 Glue on your decorations.

Sew some thread though the top of the shape.

5

Knot the ends together.

Blanket stitch This stitch looks great and is easy to do, but keep it neat!

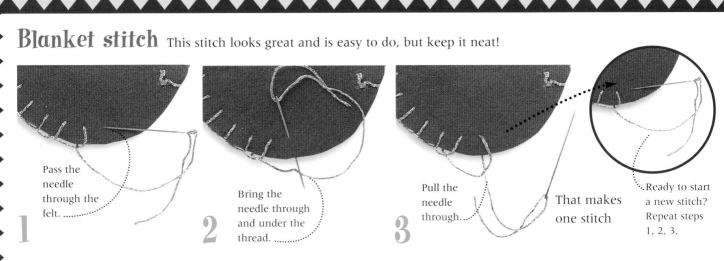

1 Pass the needle through the felt.

2 Bring the needle through and under the thread.

3 Pull the needle through...

That makes one stitch

Ready to start a new stitch? Repeat steps 1, 2, 3.

Frosty Welcomes

Light up the night before Christmas with shining ice decorations or glistening ice-bowl lanterns.

They're illuminating!

Make your garden glow
with Christmassy candlelight

157

HOW DOES YOUR GARDEN GLOW?

All you need for a Christmas glow is some seasonal cuttings, candles, and lots of ice. You can use anything wintery for your foliage, from holly and ivy to berries and cranberries—just get outside, get picking, and create a welcoming light outside in your garden.

⭐ The Big Freeze

Position a small bowl inside a larger one and tape it so that it is hanging in the center—not touching the bottom or sides. Fill the larger bowl with foliage and water, and freeze it.

If the small bowl bobs up too much put some pebbles in it to weigh it down.

⭐ Defrost Tip

To remove the bowls, you may hav to dip the frozen lantern in warm water, and pour a little into the smaller bowl as well, to loosen the

⭐ Ice Light

Use half a plastic bottle and a cup for the long lanterns, making sure that the cup doesn't touch the edges of the bottle at all. Use small or tall candles for the inside and if it starts to defrost, perk it up by putting it back into the freezer for a while.

Ask an adult...

⭐ to light the candles

1

Tape the containers

2

Drop in the plants

Let it all hang out in the garden

Tape the string to the sides of the lid to stop it from moving while it freezes.

Ice Art

Find a lid or a tray with at least a 1/2 in (1 cm) tall rim and fill it with water. Put your plant decorations into it then drape the ends of a long piece of string in either side—they will freeze with the ice and can be used to hang it up.

Fill up with water

4

Freeze it all up

5

Let it glow

Cards and Presents

Perfect for
family and friends

Greetings

From the 3rd Dimension

Bouncing Rudolphs, sticking-out snowmen, leaping stars, and a Santa bearing a bouncing gift.

They're out of this World!

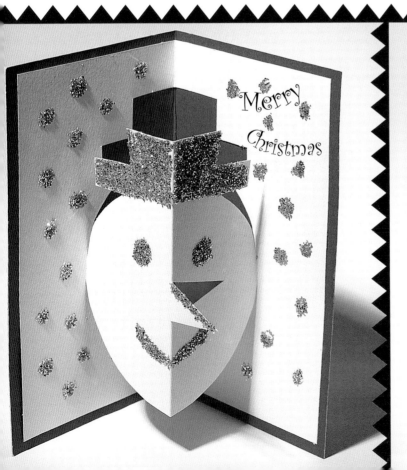

Merry Christmas

Happy holidays

HOW TO MAKE 3-D GREETING CARDS

Make sure your card is the first to be noticed on the mantlepiece with these pop-up, springing, bobbing, greeting cards!

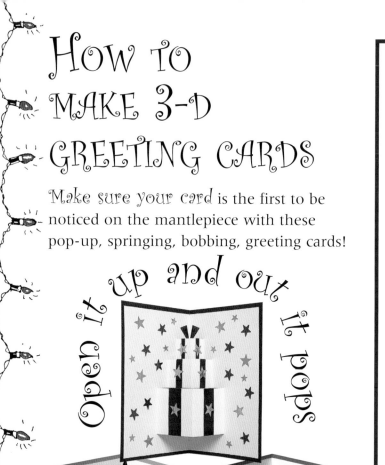

Open it up and out it pops

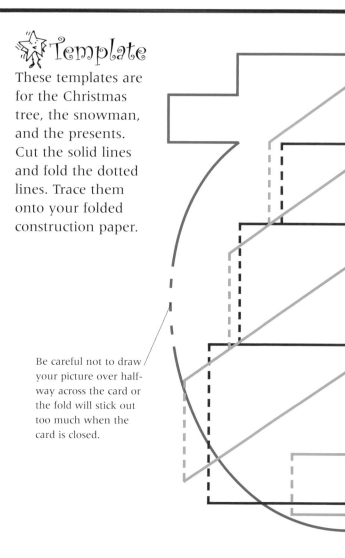

⭐ Template

These templates are for the Christmas tree, the snowman, and the presents. Cut the solid lines and fold the dotted lines. Trace them onto your folded construction paper.

Be careful not to draw your picture over half-way across the card or the fold will stick out too much when the card is closed.

⭐ 3-D, Festive, Fold-out Card

From a flat card to a pile of presents in a Christmas flash! Four simple cuts and your greeting cards are transformed. Try the snowman and Christmas tree designs, too.

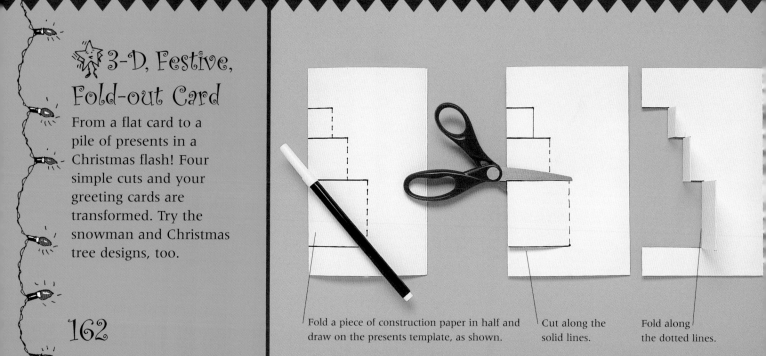

Fold a piece of construction paper in half and draw on the presents template, as shown.

Cut along the solid lines.

Fold along the dotted lines.

Pop-up Wobble Card

With this magic spring card, you can make anything appear to jump out at the person who receives it— from Rudolph's nose to Santa's present or a twinkling star. Try out some of your own designs. How about some springing, jangling bells, or a snowman spring?

Rudolph's nose

Cut out a piece of construction paper and fold it in half.

Cut Rudolf's face and nose out of two other colors of paper. Glue the face onto the main card.

Help Rudolph's nose wibble and wobble!

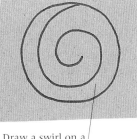

Draw a swirl on a piece of construction paper—no bigger than Rudolph's nose—and cut it out.

Glue the center of the spring to the back of the nose.

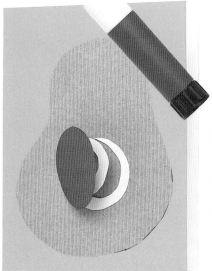

Glue the other end of the spring to Rudolph's face.

Complete Rudolph by drawing on his features.

Cut out some construction paper, slightly bigger than the original cut-out one.

Glue the construction paper to the backing piece, matching the folds in the middle.

Decorate the card with stickers or colored foil.

1 Stick it down on one side.

2 Now glue the other end of the zigzag.

3 Close the card.

4 Both sides should now be stuck on the inside so when you open it, the tutu will pop up.

5

Concertina ballerina
Fold a strip of poster-board into a zigzag as shown in step 1. Then glue one end.

Accordion cards
It's always great to get a card, especially if it's homemade. For someone really special, try making a 3-D card! Create the concertina ballerina.

Crafty cards
Using the crafty ideas in this book.

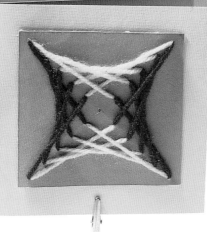

Comic card

Fold up a comic page and snip a few holes out of it, open it up, and stick it on a card!

Woolly web card

Your woolly webs are perfect patterns to stick onto cards.

Cross-stitch A B C

Use the initial of the person you are sending the card to and cross-stitch it.

Gift tags

Homemade tags finish off a present perfectly. Cut a tag out of posterboard, make a hole in the end, and tie a ribbon through it. Write on the tag or decorate it first.

Giving gifts

The tissue-paper roses on page 50 make lovely gifts. Pop one into a vase or turn several into a rose tree by putting them into a plastic cup. To do this, place a piece of sticky tack in the bottom of the cup and firmly push the straw stalk into it. Decorate the outside and give it as a present.

Three paper roses

Green tissue paper

Glue a piece of tissue paper around the cup and snip the edges.

Paper roses

The paper roses can also be stuck flat on a card or tag.

Special delivery

Cards and envelopes can be made from your own printed paper— or any paper you choose.

Aunt Daisy
4567 Garden Avenue
East Rosebud

Homemade envelopes

When you have made your cards, sometimes it's difficult to find the perfect-sized envelope to fit them. Your best bet is to make one yourself. You can even make it to match your card.

Measure your card to make sure it will fit in the envelope.

Take a square piece of paper and fold the left and right corners into the middle.

Fold the bottom corner up to the middle.

Fold the top flap down last, and when you have put a card inside, use a sticker to seal it.

To **Mom**

Dad

Grandma
123 Needle Street
Knittsville

Make envelopes out of
magazines, comics, wrapping
paper, or even brown paper.

For an even simpler
envelope, take a
rectangular piece of
paper and fold it into
three sections.

Unfold it and glue the
edges of the bottom
section.

Fold the top flap down.

Use a sticker to seal
the envelope down.

Write your
addresses on
sticky labels.

Potted presents

Painted pots make perfect presents. Put a plant in a pot, pop on the lid, and tie it up with a ribbon.

Pot luck

Fill a pot with everything someone will need to plant their very own mini garden.

1 Use acrylic paint, or poster paint mixed with white glue, to decorate a plant pot.

2 Fill it with goodies. You could provide a bag of potting mix, a bag of gravel, a seed packet of your choice, and a painted pebble with a picture of the flower that will grow on it as a label.

3 Cut a ribbon into two long pieces and lay them in a cross shape. Place the pot in the middle and tie them in a bow across the top.

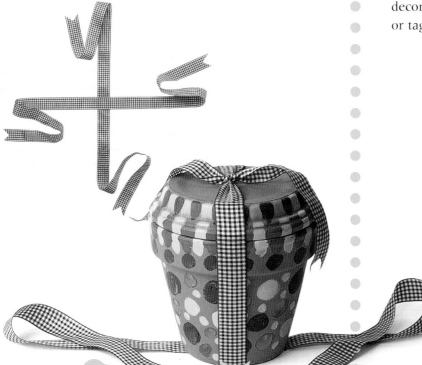

4 Finally, attach a decorated label or tag to it.

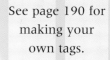
See page 190 for making your own tags.

Secret snowman

Surprise, surprise! What's Frosty hiding under his hat?

Secret snowballs

They're not just a pretty decoration to hang on the tree, but a secret stash of goodies. Give one to a friend and fill it with gifts.

Pull your snowball apart

...and let the goodies roll out

Off with his hat!
Look what's inside...

Make a paper pot

WHITE GLUE

TORN-UP NEWSPAPER

BALLOONS

To stop the paper from sticking to the balloon, spread petroleum jelly on it.

1

Cover the balloon with white glue.

2

Spread pieces of newspaper over the balloon, leaving the bottom uncovered.

3

Repeat steps 1 and 2 six more times. Finish with a layer of white glue.

4

Leave it to dry for a day or two.

Use a jar to support it.

Pop!

When it's hard and dry, pop the balloon.

Make a secret snowman

You will need to start with two pots the same size. That means you will have to blow up your balloons to match. One will be for the hat and the other for the head.

2

HAT

HEAD

Trim them down

1

The dotted lines show where to trim them down.

First make two pots

Paint and PVA

Mix equal amounts of paint with PVA (white) glue. This gives a nice sheen when dry and makes the pot stronger.

FOLD ALONG DOTTED LINES

Nose template

Trace this nose shape and cut it out of card.

3

Wrap it in masking tape.

Scrunch up some paper into a ball.

Use a strong glue to fix it in place.

Trim the hat

4

Stick on a folded paper nose with strong glue.

Paste some pieces of paper over the seams.

Add a nose

5

Paint them with white paint mixed with white glue.

Leave them to dry.

Paint them all white

6

Mix the paints with white glue.

Give him a face

Make a bauble

Make two pots and this time blow up two smaller balloons to the same size.

1 Make two small pots.

2 Trim them down.

Cover with white paint.

BASE POT   POT LID

3 Ask an adult to make a small hole in the bottom of each pot.

4 Decorate the pots with paint and glitter.

5 Take a piece of ribbon 22 in (60 cm) long and tie the two ends together.

Pass the ribbon up through the hole in the large pot.

Push the ribbon through the hole in the lid and now you can hang it up.

A Winter Wonderland

Who would ever know

that these Christmassy characters in their wintery lands are more than just great-looking faces? Open them and see for yourself.

Hats off to penguins with presents!

Keep your head or you'll give away the secret!

Goodies Galore

Don't just build one snowman, make a whole family to guard the presents and keep extra presents safely inside. Create a forest of trees in a snowy land, filled to the brim with gifts and goodies.

The penguin and snowman chat happily, keeping their secrets under their hats!

HOW TO MAKE GIFT BOXES

Collect all sorts of tubes, big or small from potato chip canisters and cookie containers to toilet paper and paper towel rolls—all are perfect for your character boxes. The important thing is to fill them with candy, or other little gifts, and surprise someone on Christmas day.

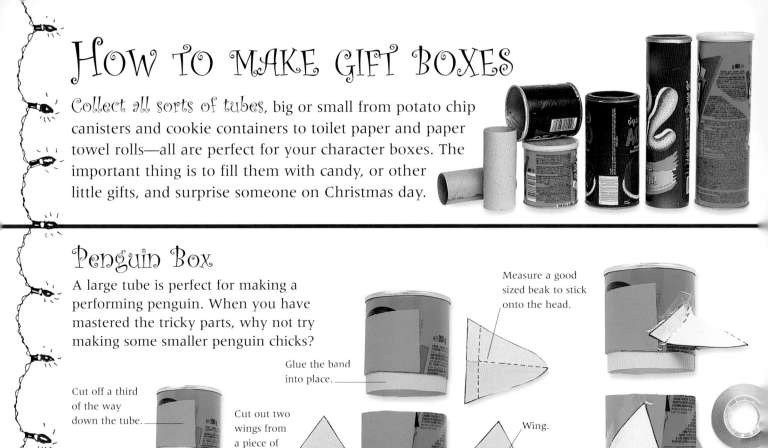

Penguin Box

A large tube is perfect for making a performing penguin. When you have mastered the tricky parts, why not try making some smaller penguin chicks?

Cut off a third of the way down the tube.

Make a cardboard band and wrap it neatly inside the top part. This will keep the lid on.

Cut out two wings from a piece of cardboard.

Glue the band into place.

Measure a good sized beak to stick onto the head.

Wing.

Cut out a penguin tail and two flappy feet.

Tape the features to the tube.

Festive Firs

Hang these trees up by their ribbons or sit them in a foresty lineup. Why not put them around the base of a Christmas tree?

Cut a semicircle of paper to make a cone big enough for your container.

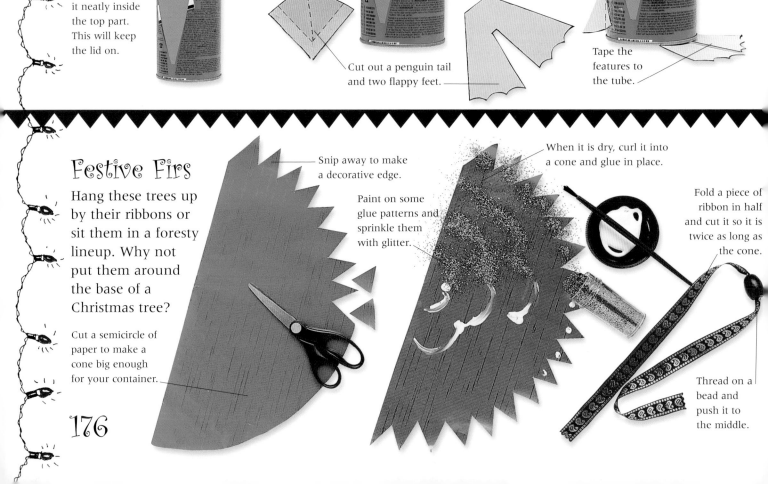

Snip away to make a decorative edge.

Paint on some glue patterns and sprinkle them with glitter.

When it is dry, curl it into a cone and glue in place.

Fold a piece of ribbon in half and cut it so it is twice as long as the cone.

Thread on a bead and push it to the middle.

176

Penguin Suit

Cut out a triangle of material.

Put glue along the edge.

Make this edge long enough to fit around the top of the head with a 1/4 in (5 mm) overlap.

Try it on your penguin and trim it until it fits. Glue the sides together.

Glue the hat to the tube.

Add a band and a pom-pon.

Give him some eyes.

Make clothes out of scraps of material.

Paint the penguin with acrylic paint and craft glue mixed together.

Paint the features using different colors.

Now fill up your penguin!

Dressing the Snowman

Prepare a tube in the same way as the penguin box.

Tape on pipe cleaner arms.

Spread glue on the box and cover it with tufts of cotton balls.

Put a ribbon through the lid and tape it in place.

Try making a junior snowman with a small tube.

Decorate him with material scraps.

Cover a container with wrapping paper for the trunk of the tree.

Make a small hole in the top and thread the ribbon through it.

Pierce two holes in the container and tie the two ribbon ends through them.

Snap on the lid to keep the goodies locked up.

A forest of firs . . .

. . . filled with fancies

177

Printing patterns

Take plain or colored paper and transform it into a frenzy of pattern. Go on, get printing!

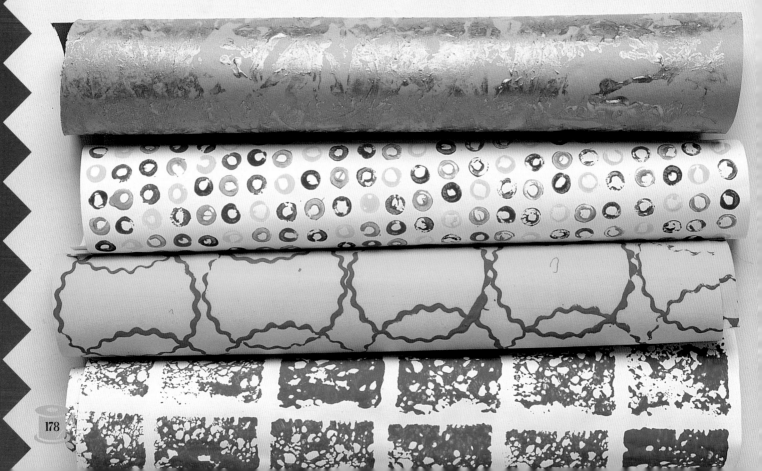

Making patterns

You will need to collect lots of paper to print on, such as brown packing paper, large sheets of plain white paper, or colored paper. The best paint to use is poster paint, but any paint you have will do. Try these babies' footprints using your hand—you could even use your own feet.

Babies' footprints

Dip your fist into some paint.

Print your fist onto the paper.

Use your fingertips for the toes.

Odds and ends

Search around the house for any items that you think would be good for printing. Remember to ask if you can cover these things in paint! Then dip them in the paint and press down on the paper.

Empty thread spools.

Pen end

Cookie cutter

Sponge

Scrunched up plastic or paper bag.

Dip the spools into the paint.

Press down onto the paper.

Plastic letters

Carved-out carrot

Bubble wrap

Carved-out potato

Pen end

Brush

Marble paper

It's so good, the technique
needs to be kept a secret!

Marble effects

Marble paper looks so
impressive that it will
astound your friends,
AND it's really easy to do.
Once you have made it,
you can wrap things in it,
cover things with it, use it
as a frame, write on it.
You'll impress everyone
you know with it!

The marble effect

Oil and water don't mix—that's how the paint stays on the surface of the water—and that's how it makes wiggly, marbly swirls on the paper. If that doesn't make sense, don't worry; just follow the instructions. You'll be amazed.

The paint mixture

Before you start, make the paint mixtur[e] Squeeze a blob of paint into a cup and a[dd] four caps full of turpentine. Mix them together. The paint will become very thi[n]

Ask an adult to help mix the paint with turpentine.

PAPER TOWEL

WHITE PAPER

COCKTAIL PICK

PAINT CUPS

TURPENTINE

BAKING TRAY WITH WATER

OIL PAINTS

NEWSPAPER

3 ## Lay the paper on it
Just let the paper float on the water.

4 ## Give it a push
Gently push the paper to help it make contact.

1 Add the paint to some water

Pour about 1 in (3 cm) of water into the tray. Add a small teaspoon of each color paint mixture.

2 Swirl the paint around

Dip a cocktail pick in and move it around in the mixture, but don't mix it!

5 Remove the paper

Pick up the corners and lift the paper out quickly.

6 Let it dry

Allow it to dry flat on newspaper.

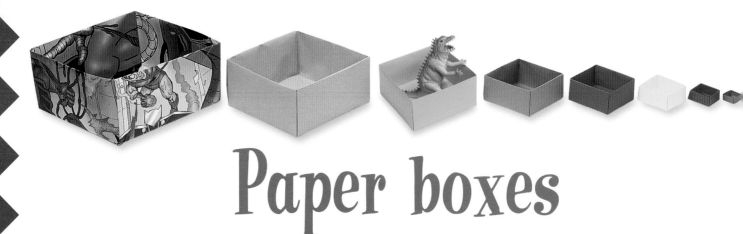

Paper boxes

What do you do if you need a box of a particular size? Simple: you make one yourself. And you can not only choose the size, you can choose the color, too. Try using wrapping paper or homemade printed paper.

Making a block box

As you make each fold, make sure you press the fold down firmly so that when you open it, you can see the crease.

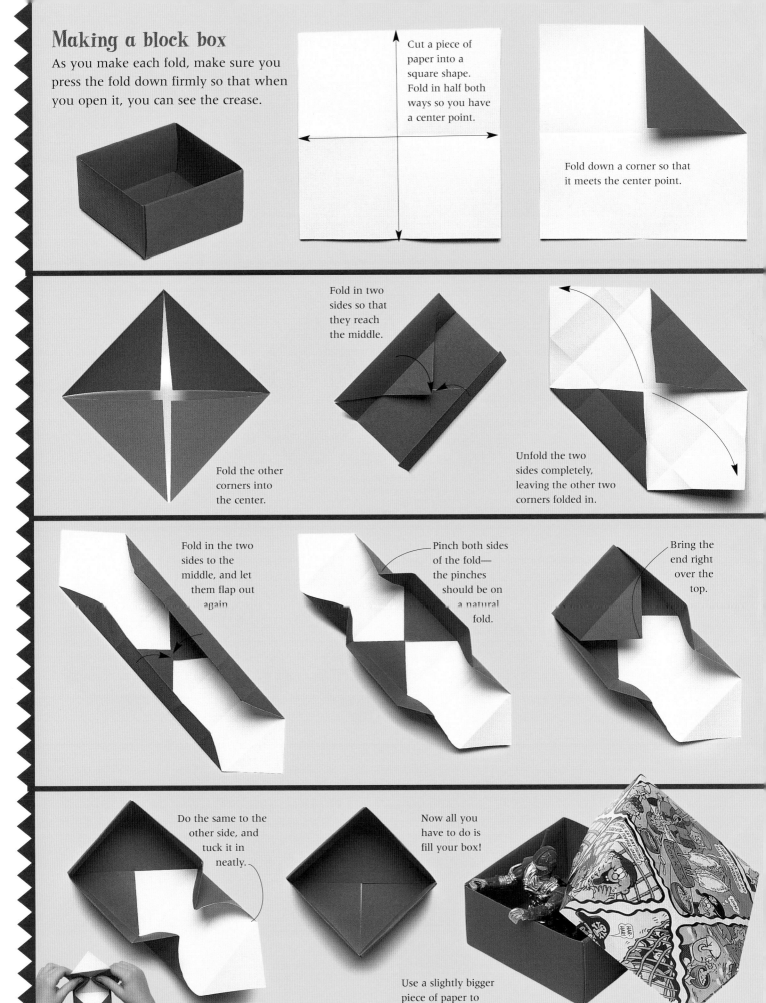

Cut a piece of paper into a square shape. Fold in half both ways so you have a center point.

Fold down a corner so that it meets the center point.

Fold the other corners into the center.

Fold in two sides so that they reach the middle.

Unfold the two sides completely, leaving the other two corners folded in.

Fold in the two sides to the middle, and let them flap out again

Pinch both sides of the fold—the pinches should be on a natural fold.

Bring the end right over the top.

Do the same to the other side, and tuck it in neatly.

Now all you have to do is fill your box!

Use a slightly bigger piece of paper to make a lid.

A star box

Stuff your star full of candies and other delicious little fancies.

To start with...

fold a square piece of paper...

along these folds...

then unfold them again.

Hold the top and bottom corners, and bring them together, making sure you tuck the two sides in.

The opening should be at the top.

It should be a diamond shape with two flaps in the middle.

Make sure the opening is at the top.

Fold one side along to the central fold.

Open up the small flap and press flat.

Make sure these two folds line up.

Tuck the left side of the small flap behind itself.

Now do the same to the other side.

Both sides should now look the same.

Turn it over so that the other side is showing.

The back should look exactly the same as the front.

Do the same with the flaps at the back.

Fold all four flaps down as far as they will go.

When you have folded two flaps down, pull the other two to the side and they will fold down, too.

Your box should start to open when you fold over the flaps.

With your hand underneath, push up the middle and it will miraculously turn into a box.

Neaten up the star flaps and FILL IT UP!

Try different sizes and colors. You could even try making them with your own printed paper.

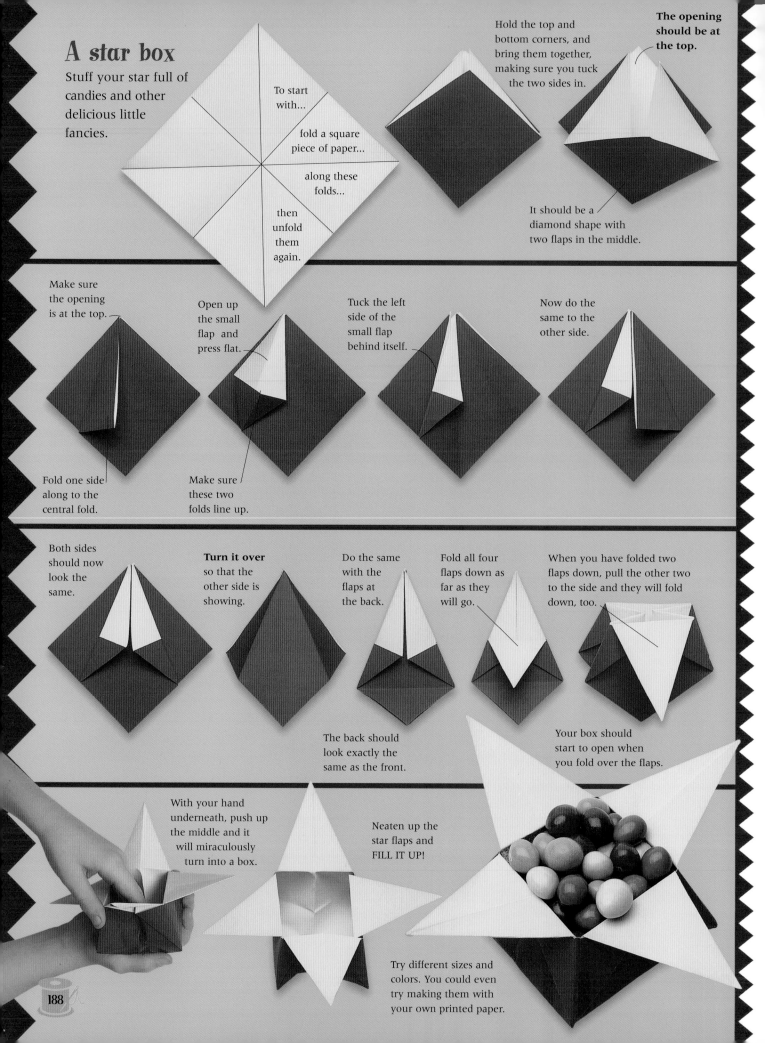

A galaxy of star boxes

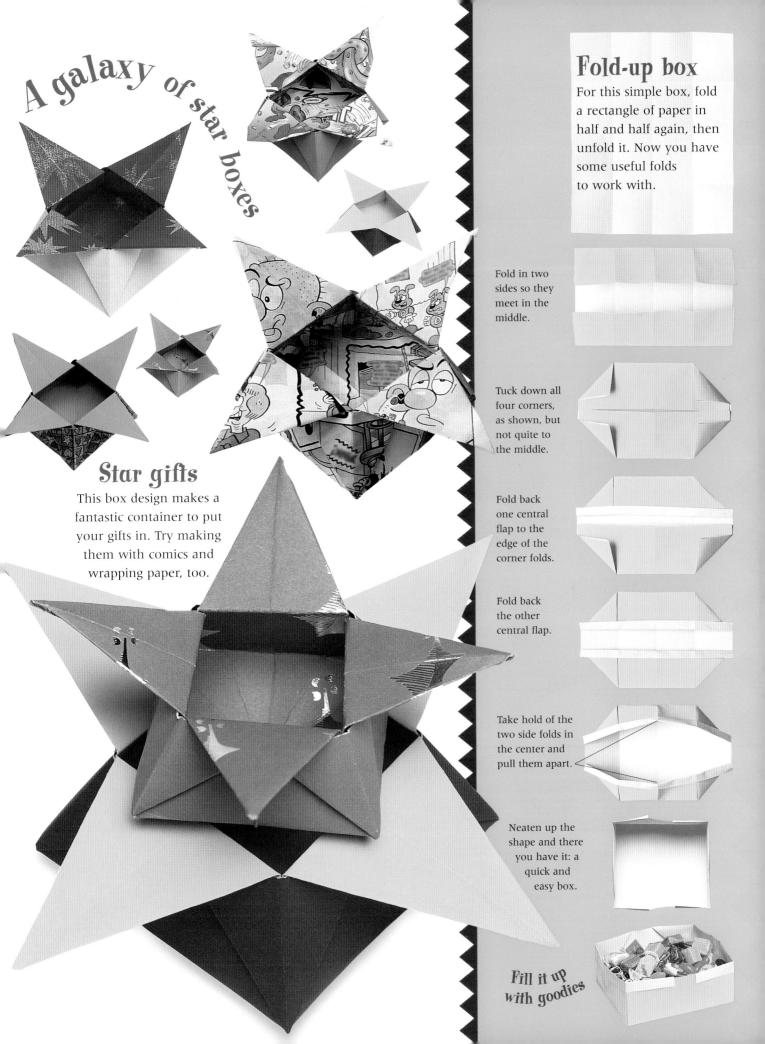

Star gifts

This box design makes a fantastic container to put your gifts in. Try making them with comics and wrapping paper, too.

Fold-up box

For this simple box, fold a rectangle of paper in half and half again, then unfold it. Now you have some useful folds to work with.

Fold in two sides so they meet in the middle.

Tuck down all four corners, as shown, but not quite to the middle.

Fold back one central flap to the edge of the corner folds.

Fold back the other central flap.

Take hold of the two side folds in the center and pull them apart.

Neaten up the shape and there you have it: a quick and easy box.

Fill it up with goodies

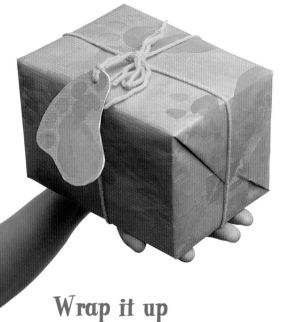

It's a wrap!

All wrapped up.

Give away your crafty projects as presents, wrapped in home-made paper with matching tags.

Tags

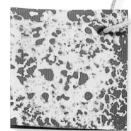

Cut out a shape and make a ho... in the corr...

Tie a pi... of ribbon... yarn thro... the hole.

Wrap it up

Take a piece of your homemade paper, and put the present in the middle.

Fold one side over the top and hold it in place.

Fold the other side over and tape in place.

Push the center of the paper down firmly.

Pull one side in and hold in place.

You could write a not... on the tag...

To Mom

or print a pattern on it.

Fold the other side in.

Fold up the triangle shape and tape in place.

To match a tag to the footprint paper, cut around the print, make a hole, and tie some yarn through it.

Homemade paper

Now you have a gift all wrapped up in your homemade, personalized wrapping paper.

Thanks, Ted! Are these all from you?

Index

Acknowledgements

With thanks to...
Stephanie Spyrakis for face painting
Maisie Armah, Eleanor Bates,
Charlotte, Billy and James Bull,
Luke Bower, Elicia Edwards,
Seriye Ezigwe, Sophie Jones,
Tex Jones, Max, Guy and Imogen
Lowery, Sorcha Lyons, Kristian
Revelle, and Kiana Smith for
craftily performing the
arty projects.

All images © Dorling Kindersley.
For further information see:
www.dkimages.com

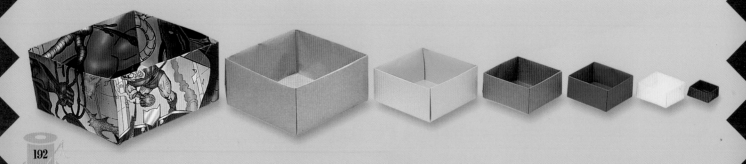